New Hamburg Ontario Book 2 in Colour Photos, Saving Our History One Photo at a Time

Photography
by Barbara Raué
2014

Series Name:
Cruising Ontario

Book 59: New Hamburg Book 2
with Haysville and St. Agatha

Cover photo: 305 Wilmot Street

New Hamburg

New Hamburg was established in the early 1830s by William Scott. In 1834, cholera killed many of the original settlers of New Hamburg. A grist-mill built by Josiah Cushman about 1834 formed the nucleus around which a small community of Amish Mennonites and recent German immigrants developed. More German and Scottish settlers arrived in the late 1830s and early 1840s. The Grand Trunk railway arrived in the 1850s and the village became an important centre for milling and the production of farm machinery.

Haysville

Haysville, where the historic Huron Road crossed the Nith River, was settled by immigrants from the British Isles in the 1830s. Robert Hays settled there and built a sawmill and grist mill. He was the first postmaster appointed in 1837 of what was then known as Wilmont. The town was renamed Haysville in 1848 in his honor. His son John succeeded him as postmaster of Haysville in 1853 and also took over the mills.

In 1827, Dr. William 'Tiger' Dunlop of the Canada Company opened the 95-mile corduroy Huron Road which connected the towns of Guelph and Goderich.

St. Agatha

As with many communities in Wilmot Township, the history of St. Agatha begins in 1824 when it was founded along Upper Road (Erb's Road) and Notre Dame Road. It is located west of Kitchener/Waterloo and northeast of New Hamburg. There are no significant creeks or rivers located in the area.

Settlers were farmers, tradesmen and shop keepers. No large scale industry was undertaken in the area. St. Agatha was settled by three German groups: Amish Mennonites, Lutherans, and Roman Catholics. Originally named Wilmot, it was changed to St. Agatha in 1852. The name St. Agatha reflected its association with the predominant Catholic parish and church of the community which was established there in the 1830s. The parish and church were named St. Agatha after the Sicilian martyr of the third century.

The earliest settlers to arrive in the St. Agatha area were Amish Mennonites from both Pennsylvania and Alsace-Lorraine who first began arriving in 1824. Other Catholic and Lutheran settlers began to arrive in the early 1830s. Wishing to continue a traditional way of life, the Amish Mennonite settlers cleared land for farming, and they cleared land along the front of their properties for the development of the Upper Road. This road led to Erb's Mills in Waterloo Township and supplies for settlement were easily acquired in the village of Waterloo. Upper Road was cleared across the township by the early 1830s.

When Roman Catholic and Lutheran settlers from Alsace-Lorraine arrived, settlers bought land from the Amish Mennonites or from the Crown directly. Many of these newcomers cleared land for the purpose of farming, but as some of the Amish Mennonite settlers migrated elsewhere within Waterloo County, Lutherans and especially Catholics came to dominate the identity of the community. Some of the Catholic and Lutheran settlers were trades workers and artisans, including blacksmiths, carpenters, shoemakers, wagon makers, and innkeepers.

In 1869, the settler population included weavers, innkeepers, blacksmiths, carpenters, masons, saddlers, and general merchants. By 1906, residents' occupations included hotel keepers, general merchants, a blacksmith, and a carriage maker.

Church life was important to the community. The Amish Mennonite community established an active congregation in St. Agatha before 1830, and erected their first meeting house in 1885. Lutheran settlers established a congregation here and built a church in 1863. Catholics organized a congregation in St. Agatha by 1834 and in 1840 a large frame church was built. It was almost completely destroyed by a storm in the same year, but was rebuilt a short time later.

The early influence of church organizations in St. Agatha contributed to the establishment of early schools. In 1834, two public log schools and a Catholic log school existed. By 1846, a stone building replaced the two public schools and in 1854, the Jesuits erected a new stone Catholic school as well. The early development of these schools in St. Agatha was well ahead of other communities within Wilmot Township, and also in Waterloo County.

Baden

Baden is a community in the Township of Wilmot in the Regional Municipality of Waterloo. It has a population of less than 1000 and was named after Baden-Baden in Germany. The Baden Tower, a huge television, radio and communications tower, is located on top of one of the Baden Hills. From here CKCO-TV transmits its signal. Much of the area consists of farmlands and there are pine forests as well. Baden was the hometown of Sir Adam Beck who pioneered hydro-electric power.

Table of Contents

New Hamburg:

	Jacob Street	Page 8
	Boulee Street	Page 19
	Church Street	Page 22
	Wilmot Street	Page 23
	Weber Street	Page 26

Holland Mills Road   Page 28

Haysville   Page 29

St. Agatha   Page

Baden   Page

Architectural Terms   Page 31
Building Styles   Page 34

New Hamburg

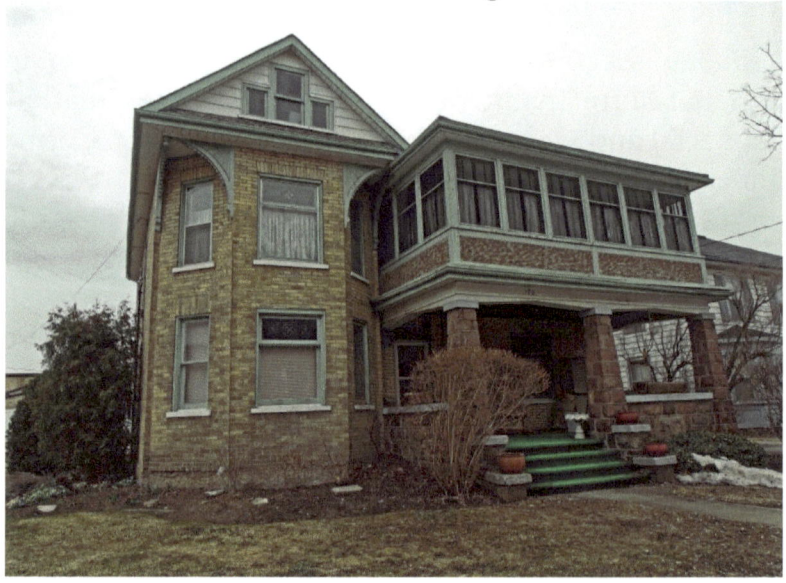

170 Jacob Street – Edwardian with Palladian window, fretwork, enclosed sunroom above verandah

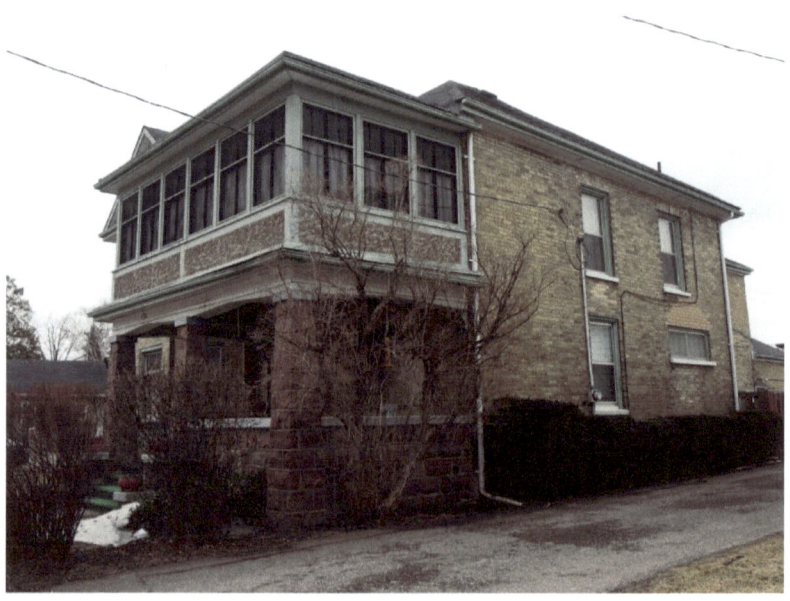

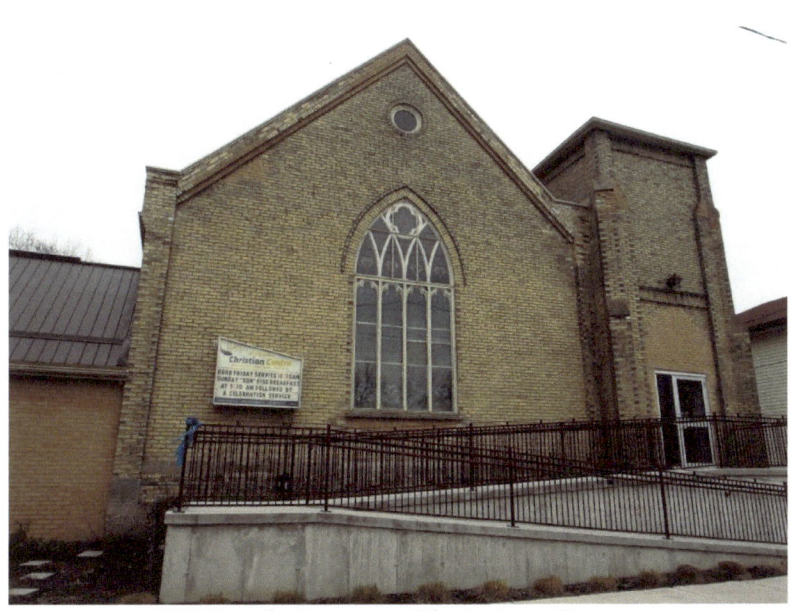

177 Jacob Street – Christian Centre
Gothic Revival

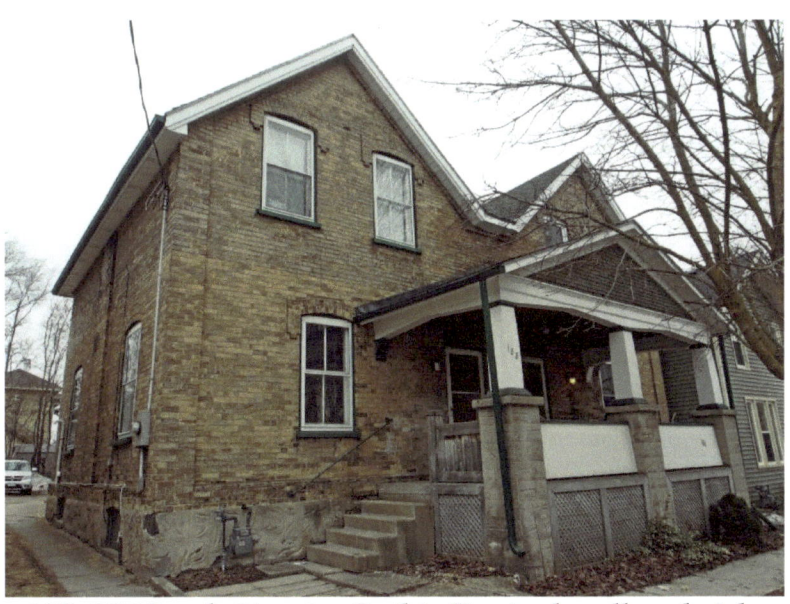

188, 186 Jacob Street – Gothic Revival, yellow brick,
pediment above verandah

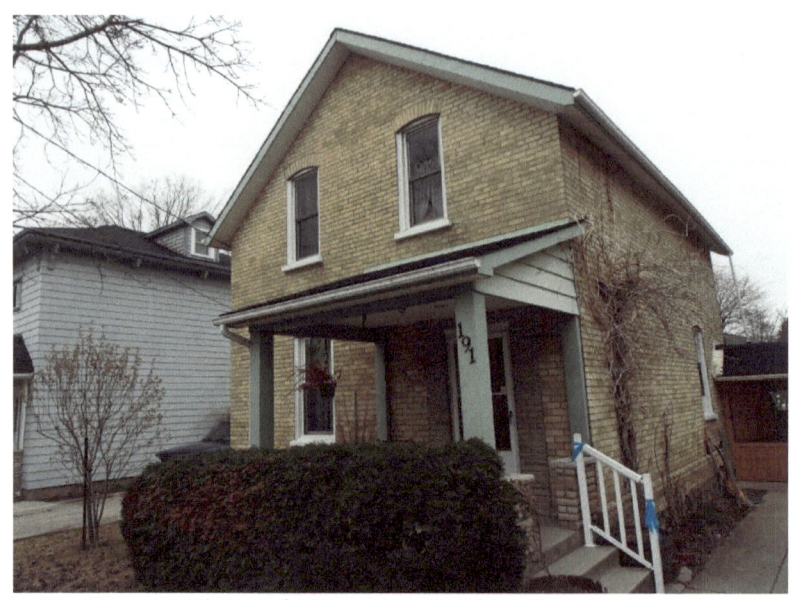

191 Jacob Street – Gothic Revival

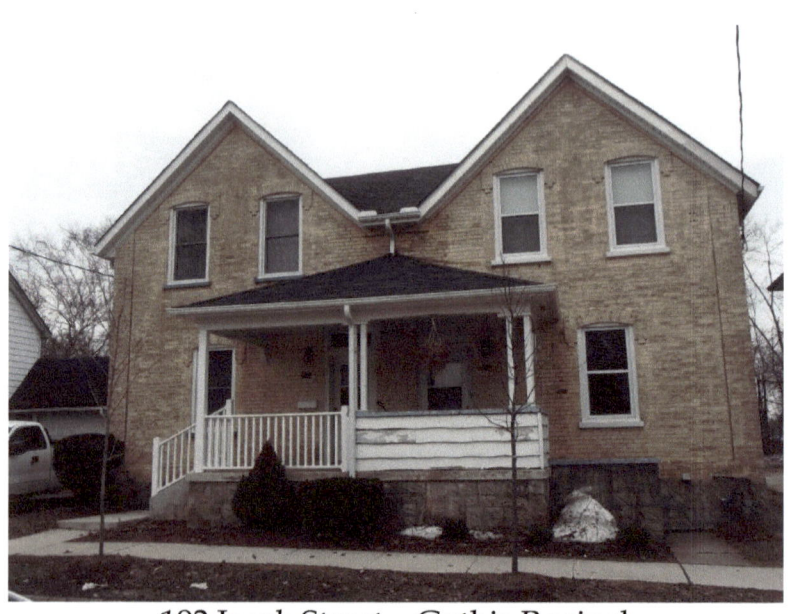

192 Jacob Street – Gothic Revival

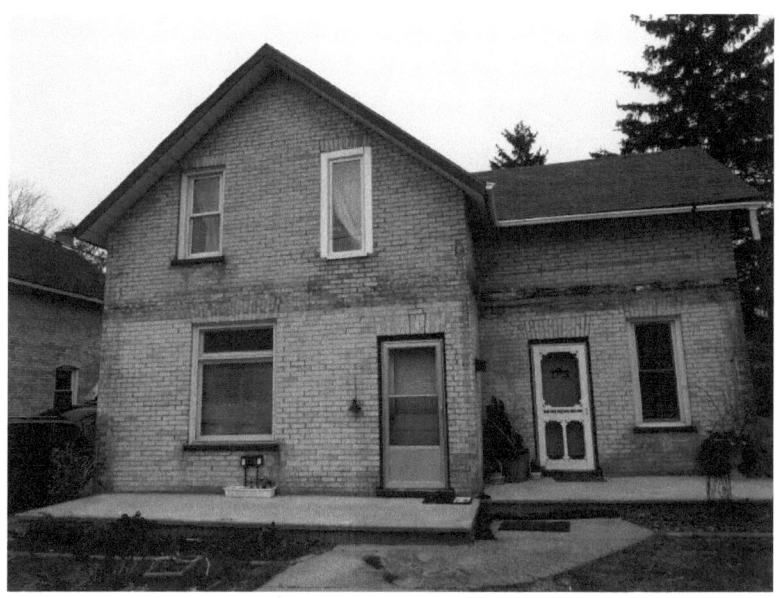

195 Jacob Street – Gothic Revival

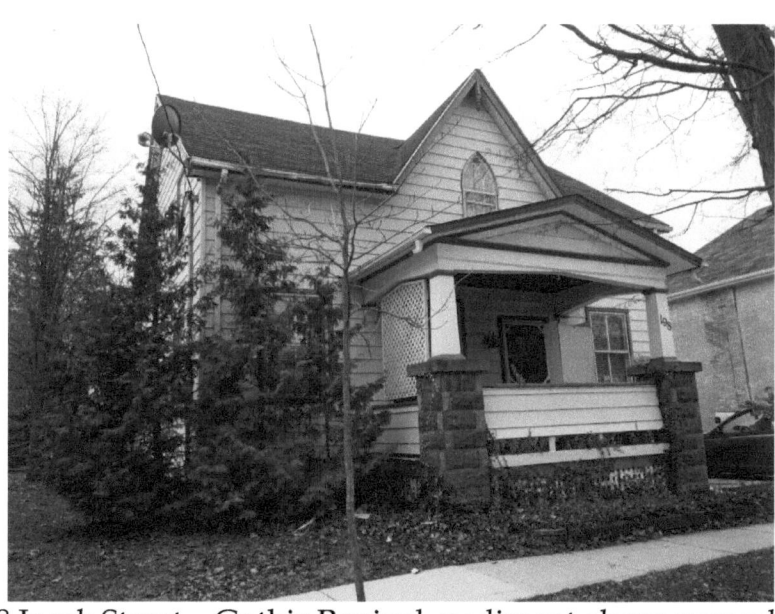

198 Jacob Street – Gothic Revival, pediment above verandah, finial on gable

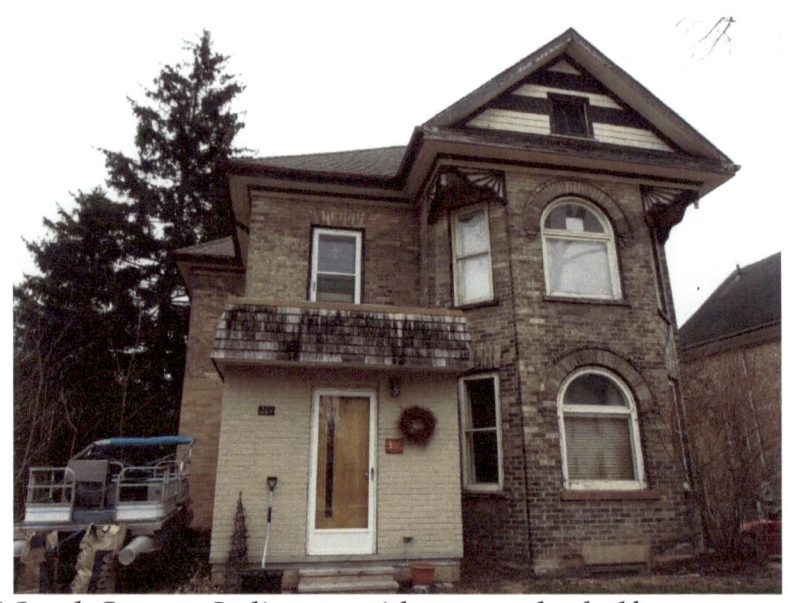

201 Jacob Street – Italianate with two-and-a-half storey tower-like bay, Romanesque style round window arches, fretwork

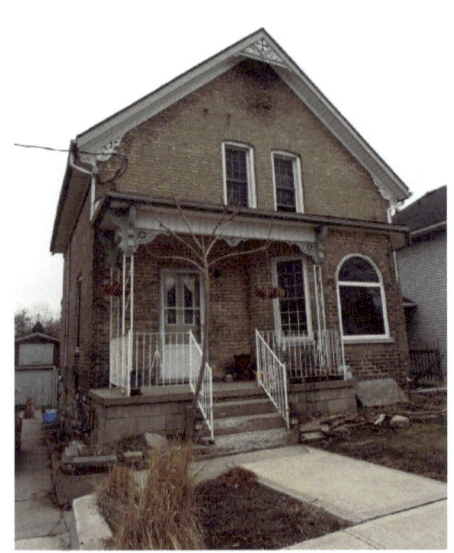

205 Jacob Street – Gothic Revival

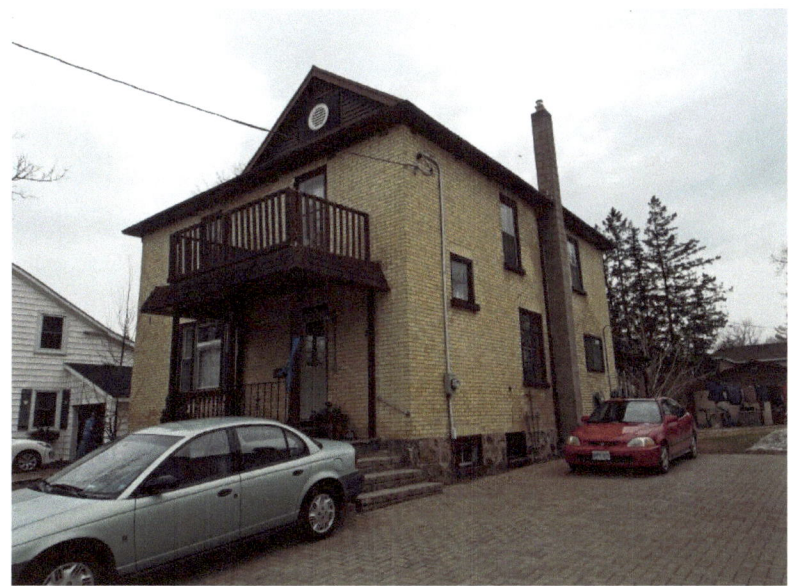

212 Jacob Street – Italianate

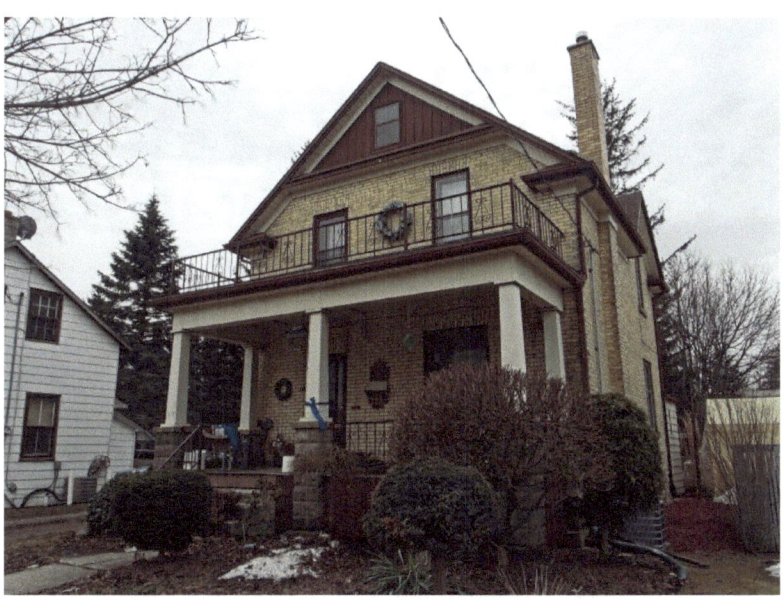

240 Jacob Street – Edwardian, balcony above verandah

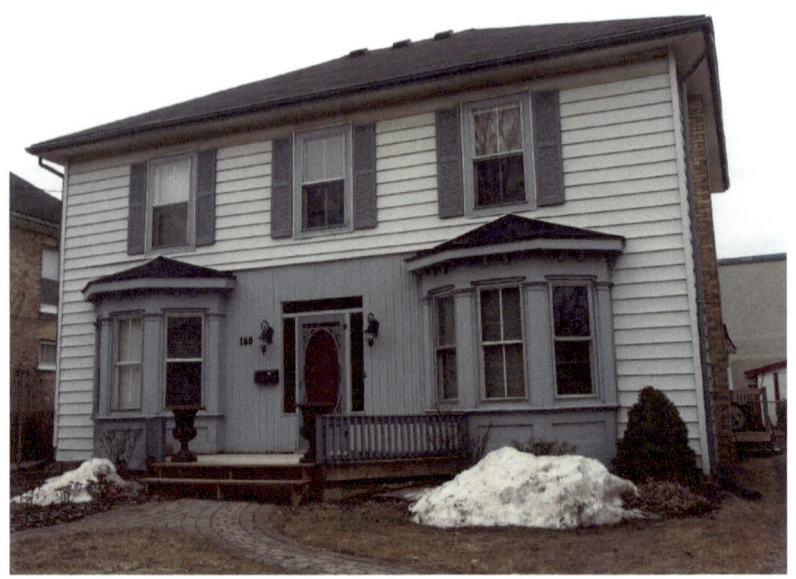

166 Jacob Street – Italianate – bay windows on ground floor, hip roof

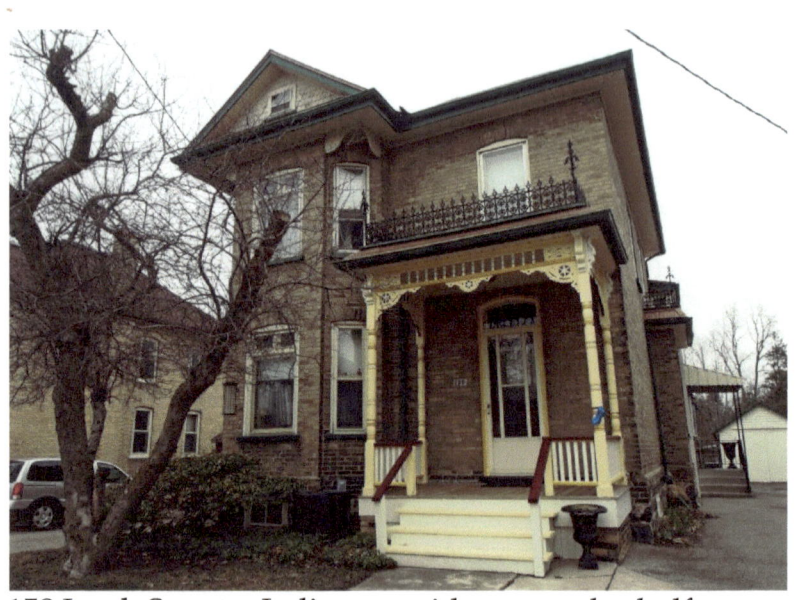

159 Jacob Street – Italianate with two-and-a-half storey tower-like bay, iron cresting above porch roof

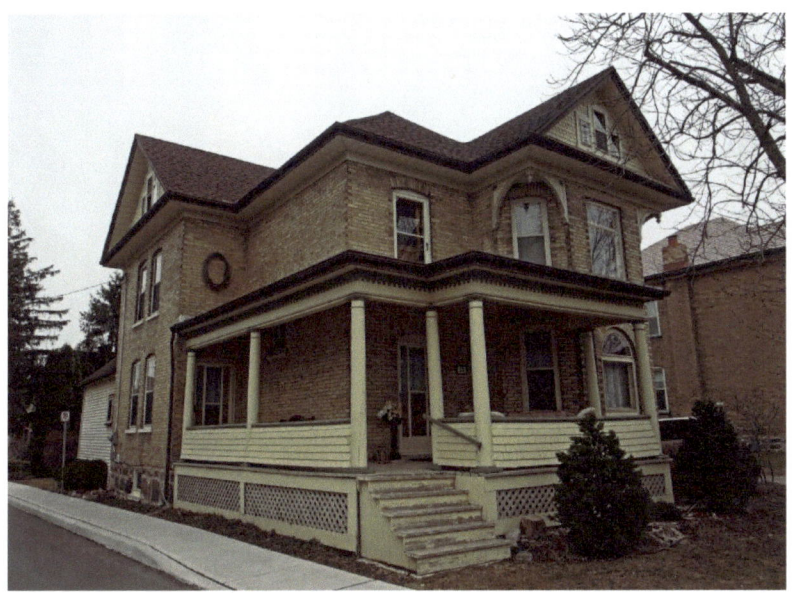

151 Jacob Street – Edwardian, Palladian windows in gables, fretwork

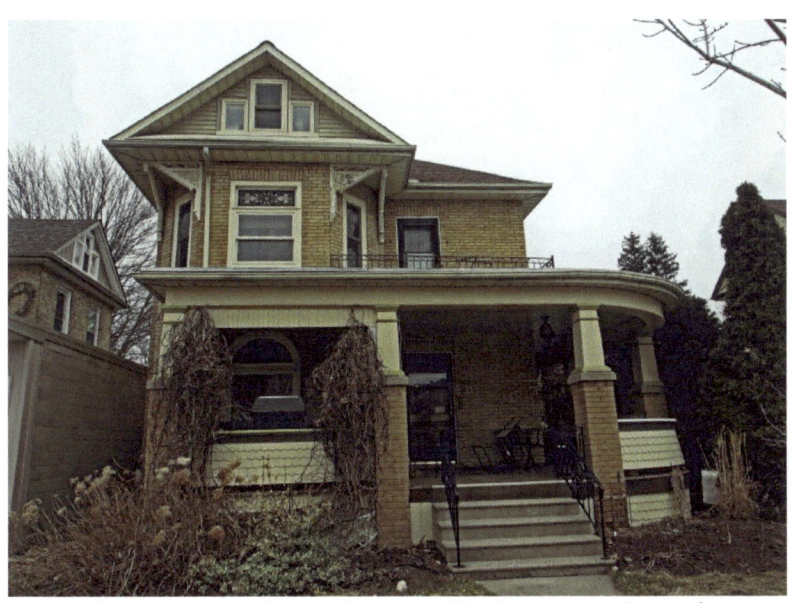

145 Jacob Street – Edwardian, Palladian window, fretwork

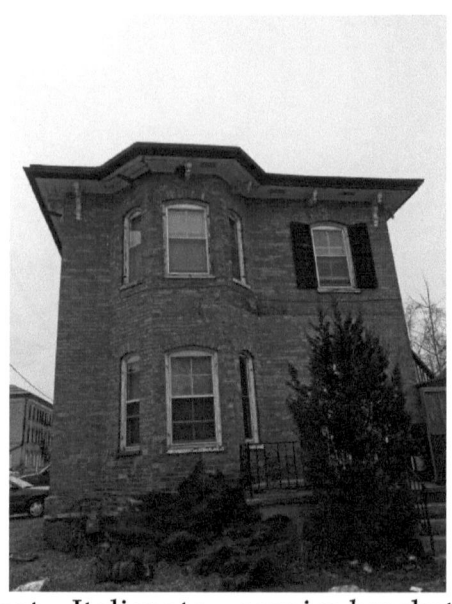

144 Jacob Street – Italianate – cornice brackets, two-storey tower-like bay, yellow brick

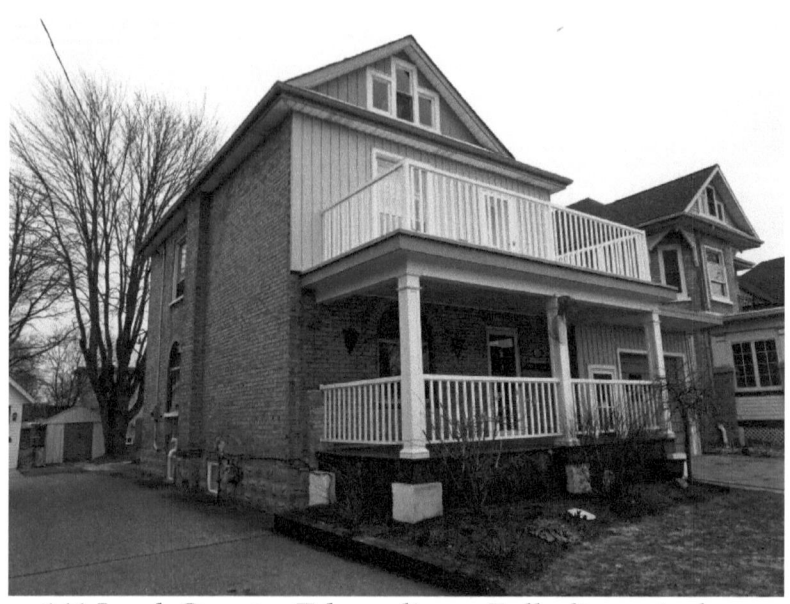

141 Jacob Street – Edwardian – Palladian window

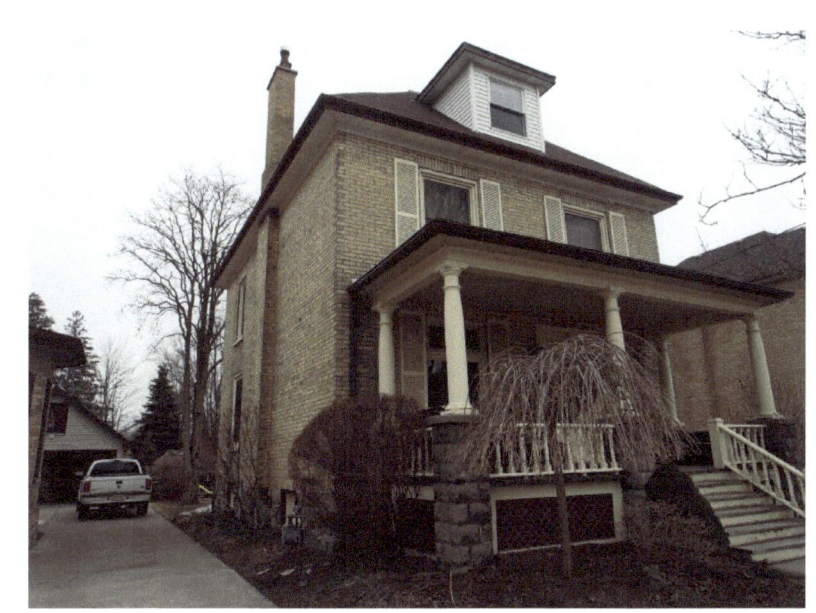

137 Jacob Street – Italianate, dormer in attic of hipped roof

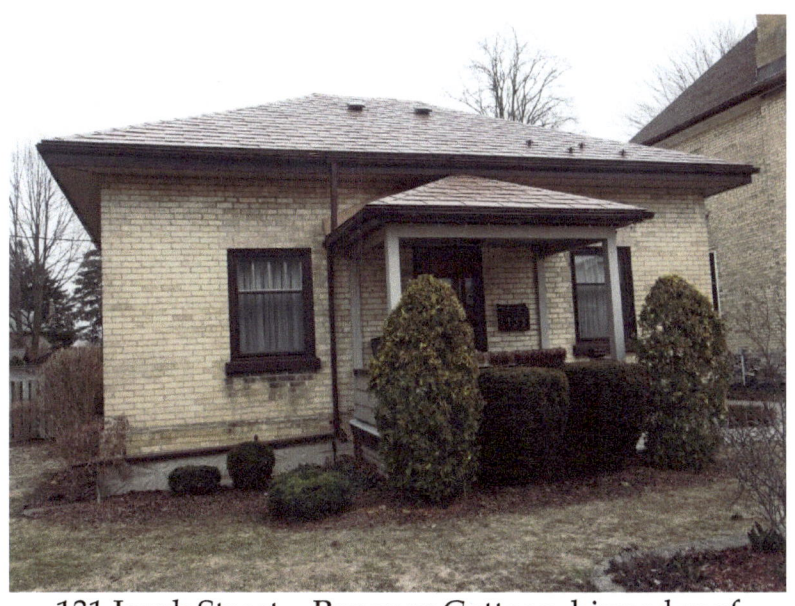

131 Jacob Street – Regency Cottage, hipped roof

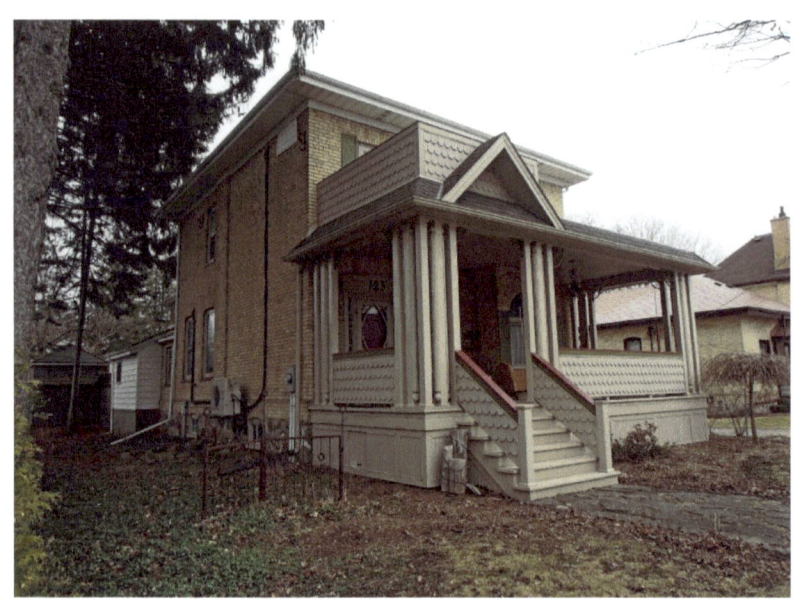

125 Jacob Street – Italianate

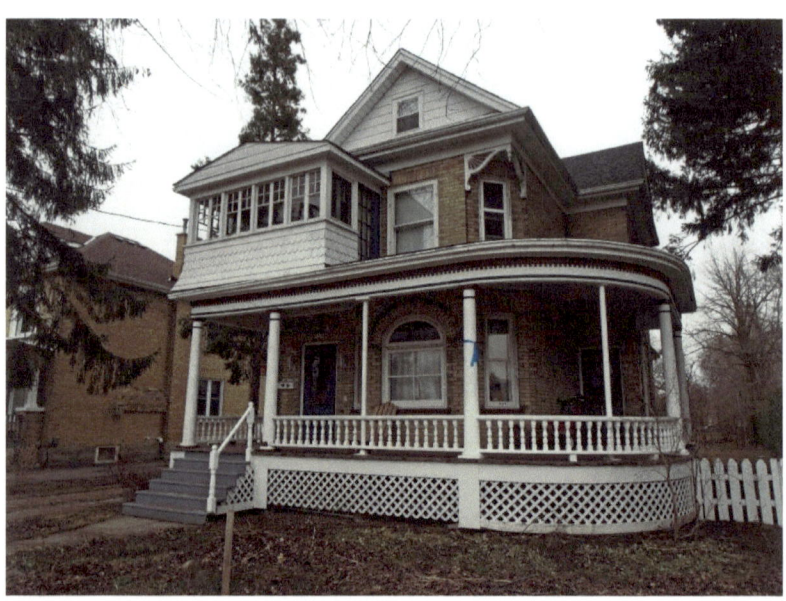

119 Jacob Street – Edwardian, fretwork, wrap-around verandah, Romanesque style round window arches, enclosed sunroom above verandah

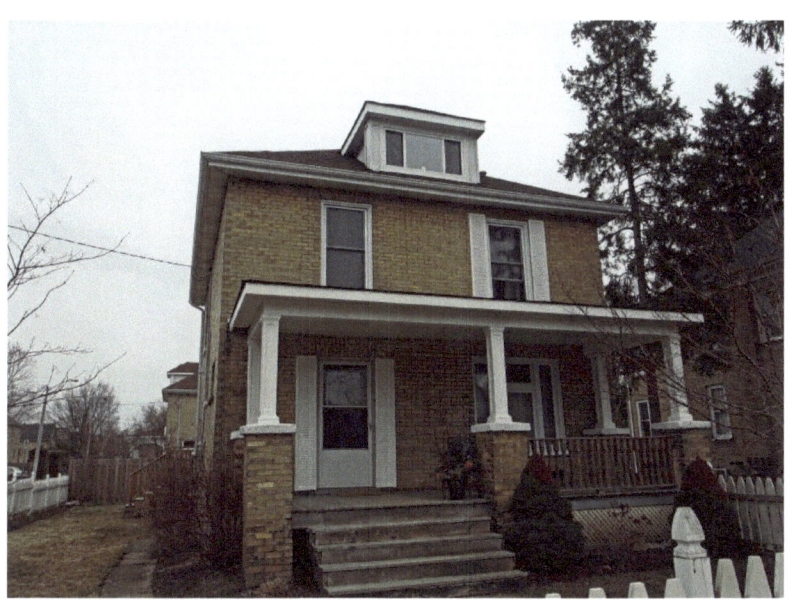

113 Jacob Street – Italianate – dormer in attic

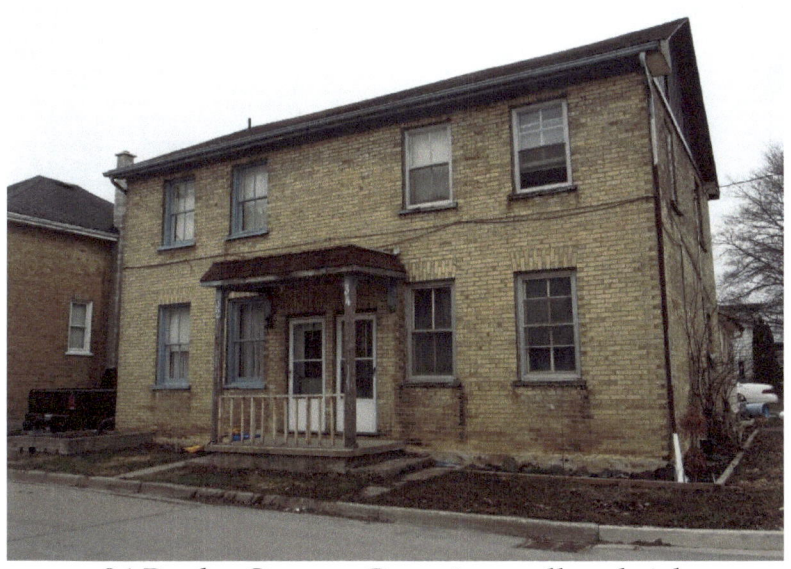

34 Boulee Street – Georgian, yellow brick

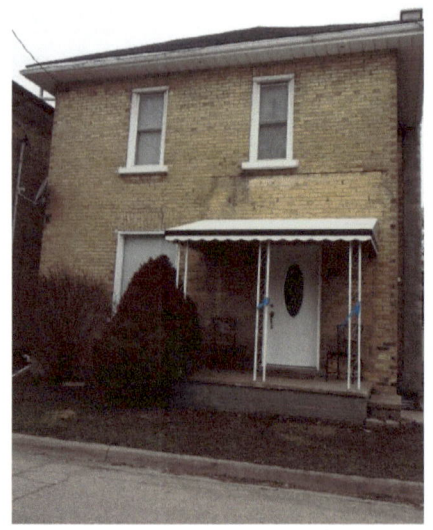

28 Boulee Street – Italianate

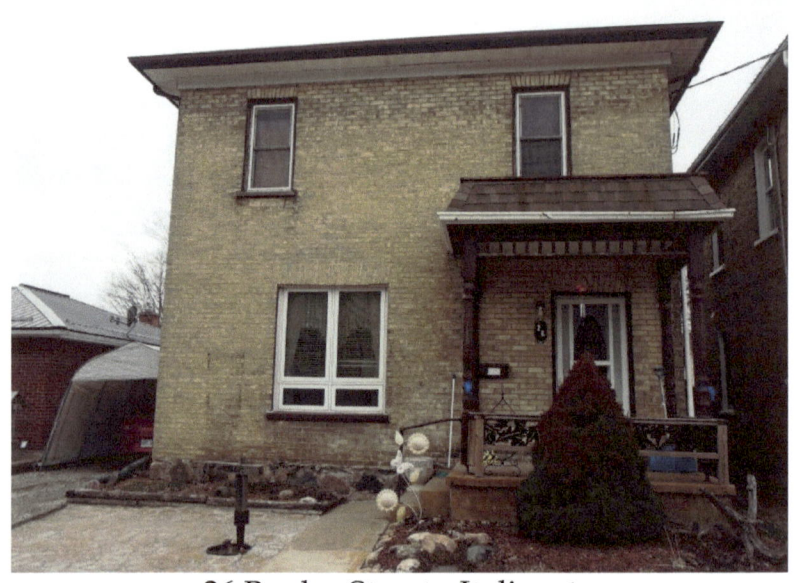

26 Boulee Street - Italianate

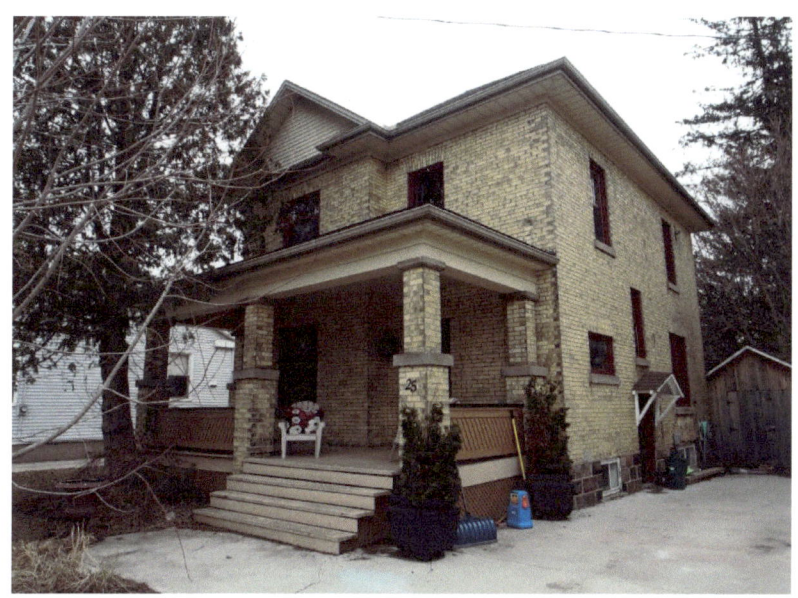

25 Boulee Street – Italianate with two-storey frontispiece topped by a gable

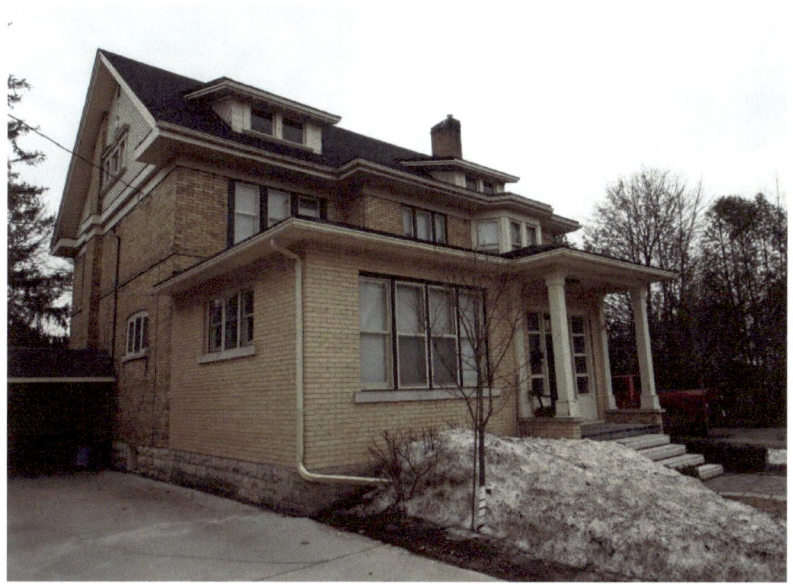

19 Boulee Street – Gothic Revival with dormers in attic

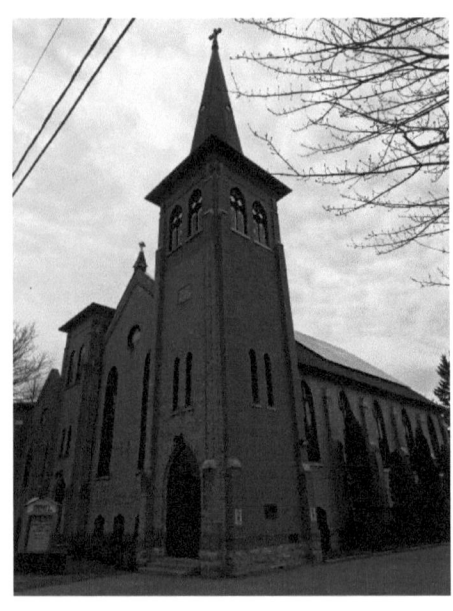

23 Church Street – Trinity Lutheran Church – A.D. 1910

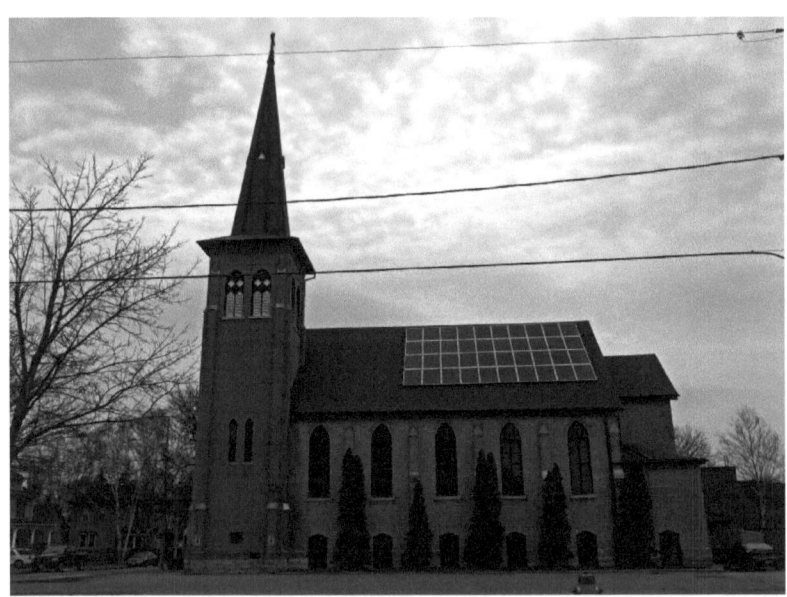

Lancet windows, buttresses

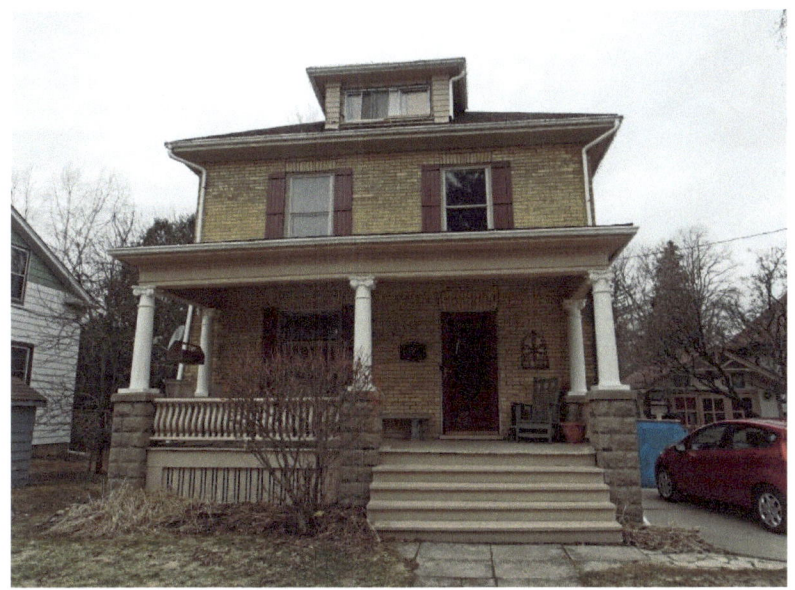

16 Church Street – Italianate – dormer in attic

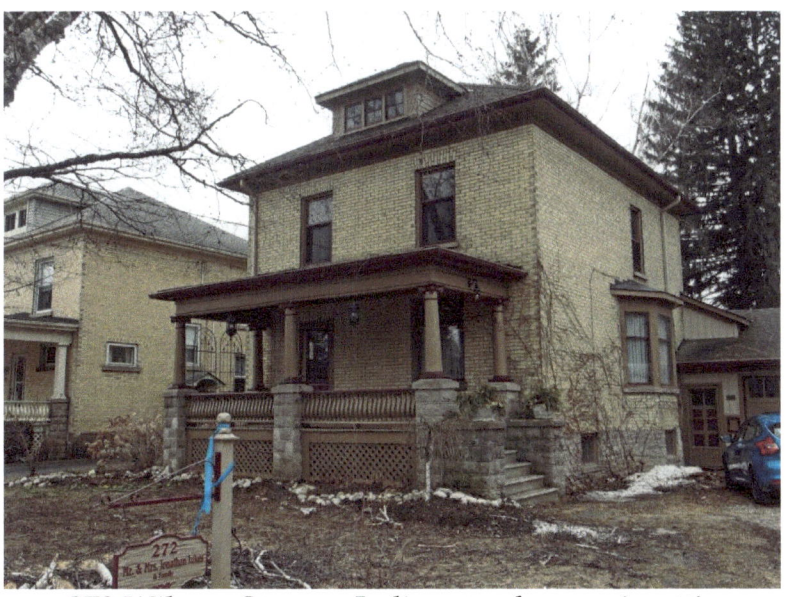

272 Wilmot Street – Italianate, dormer in attic

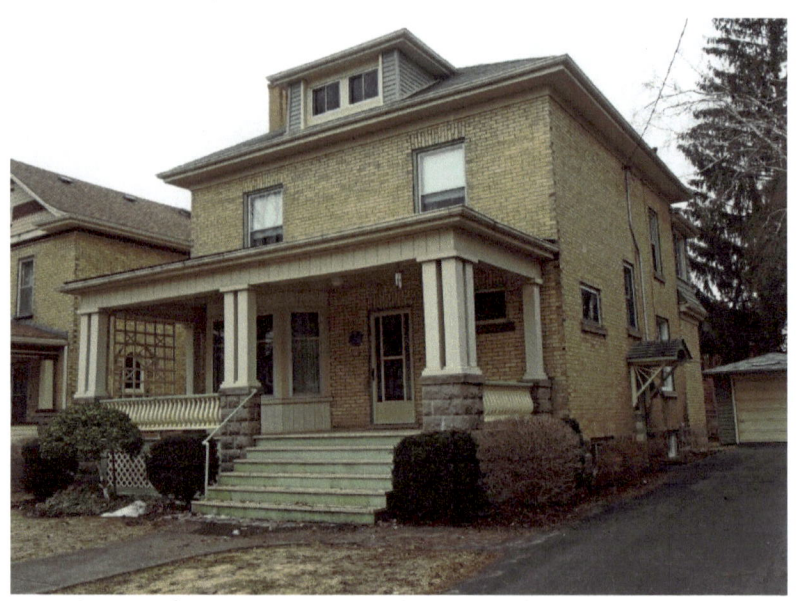

276 Wilmot Street – Italianate, dormer in attic

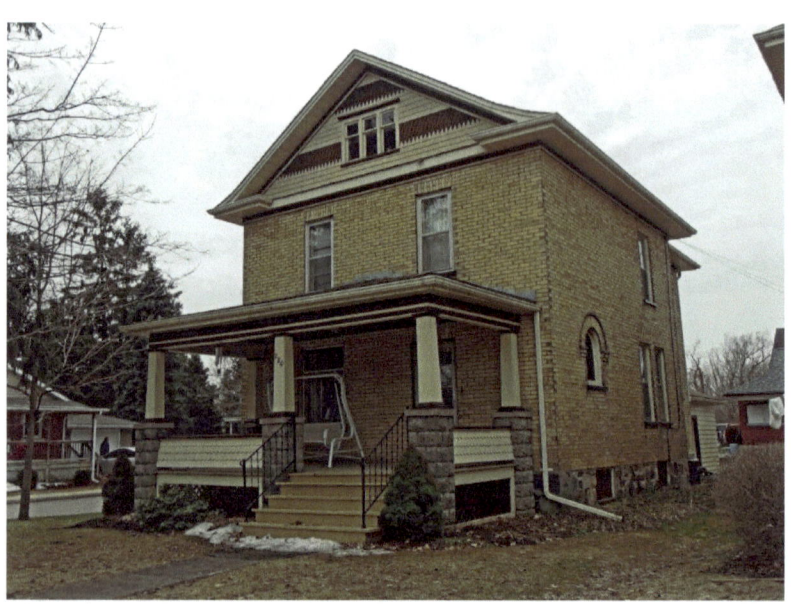

280 Wilmot Street – Edwardian, Romanesque style round window arches

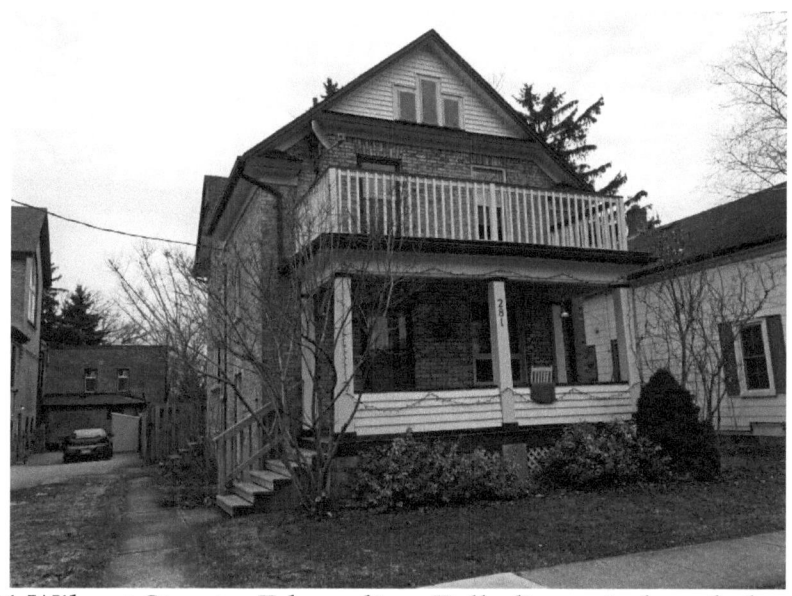

281 Wilmot Street – Edwardian, Palladian window, balcony above verandah

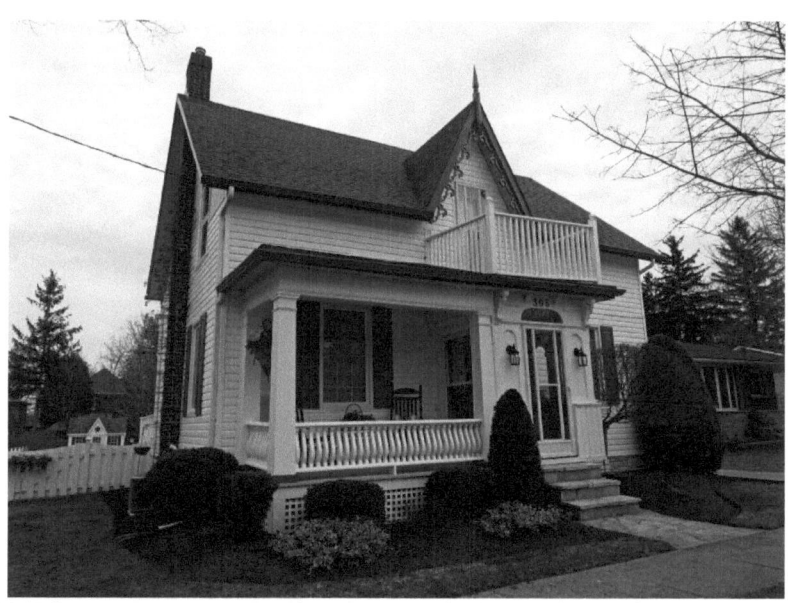

305 Wilmot Street – Gothic Revival, Vergeboard trim on gable with finial, balcony on second floor

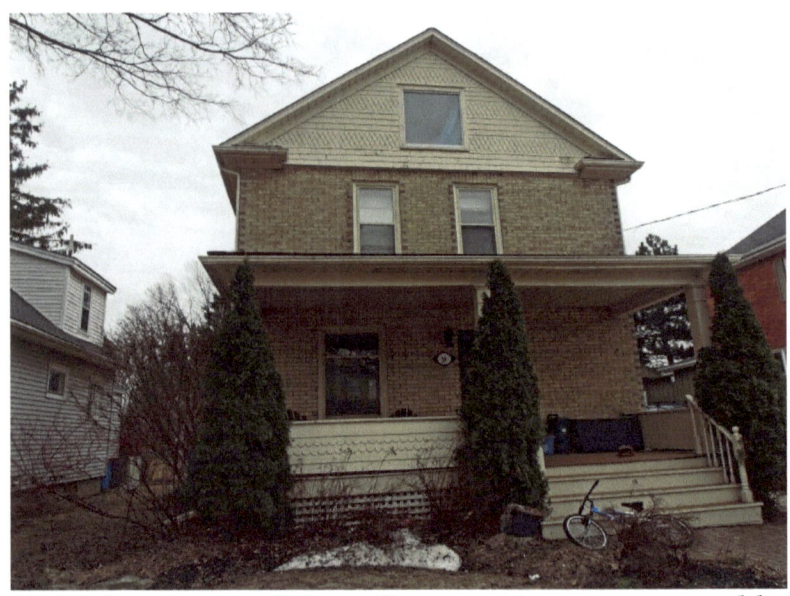

59 Weber Street – Edwardian, cornice return on gable

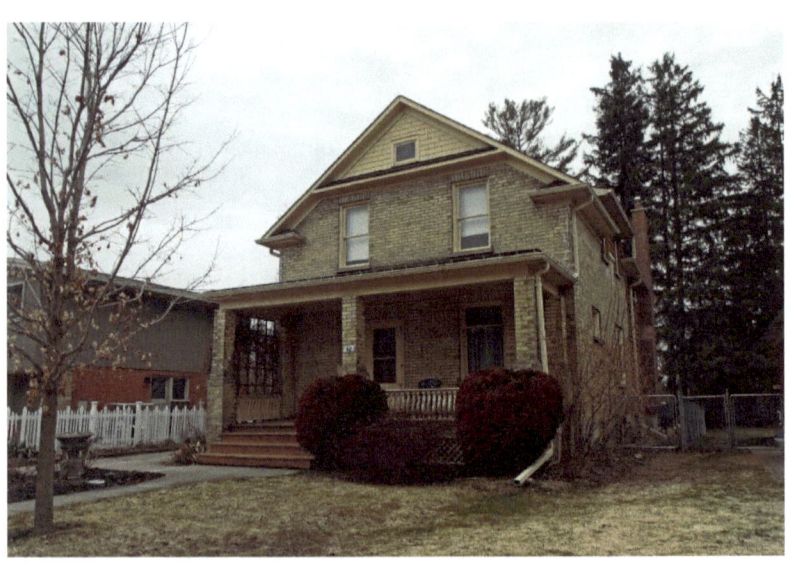

60 Weber Street - Edwardian

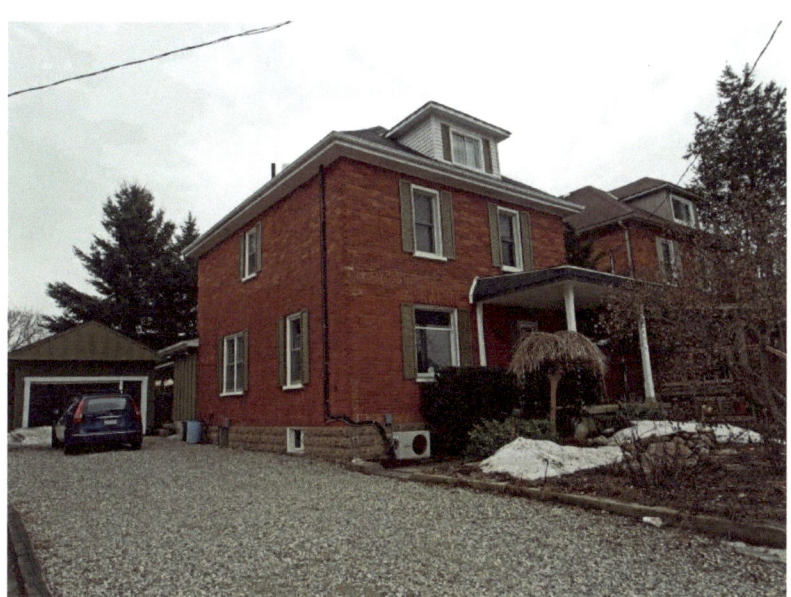

65 Weber Street – Italianate, dormer in attic

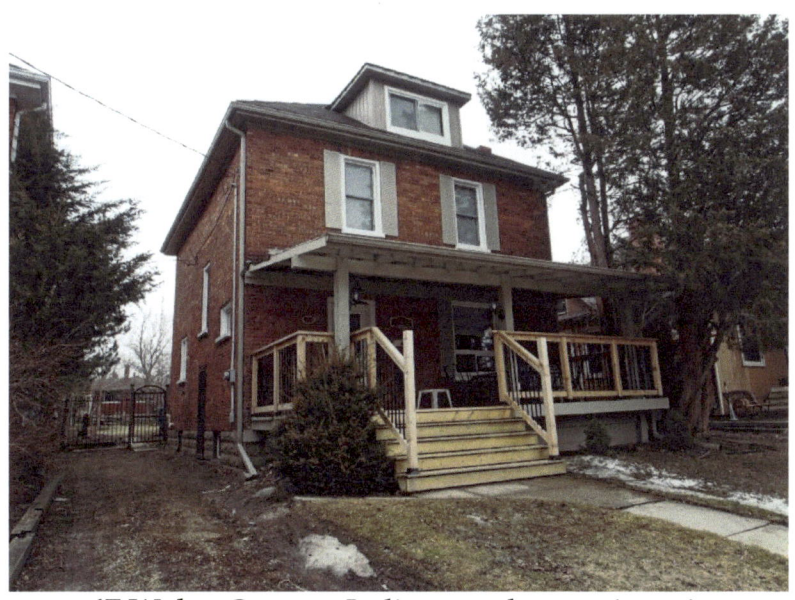

67 Weber Street – Italianate, dormer in attic

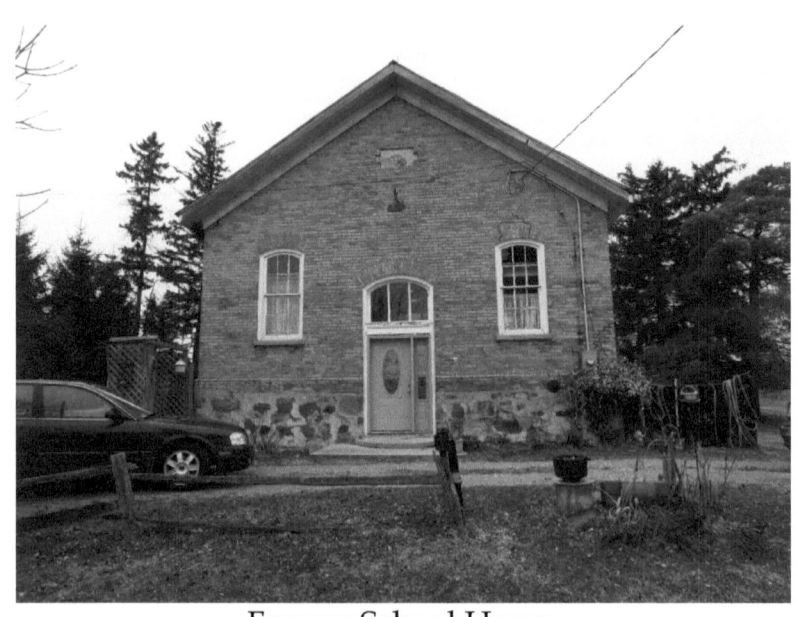

Former School House
2492 Holland Mills Road – on the way to Haysville
Gothic Revival, cobblestone basement

Haysville

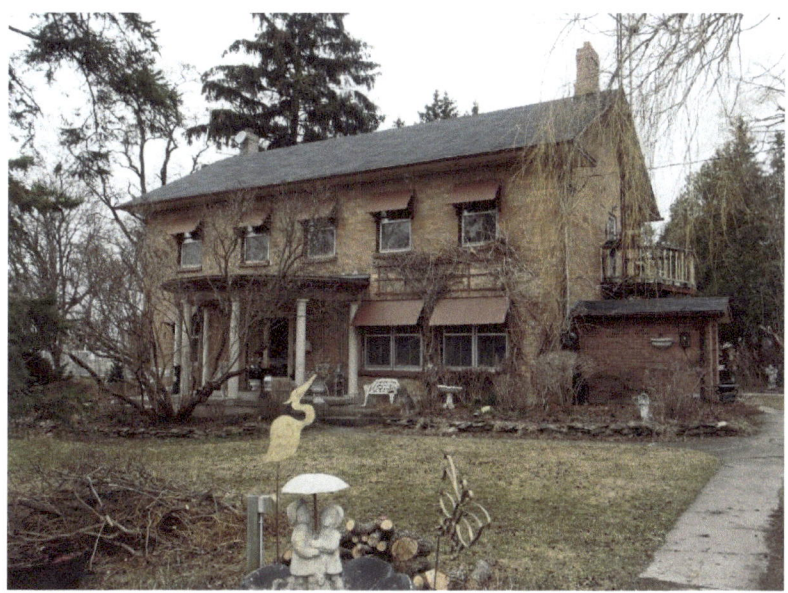

Georgian style

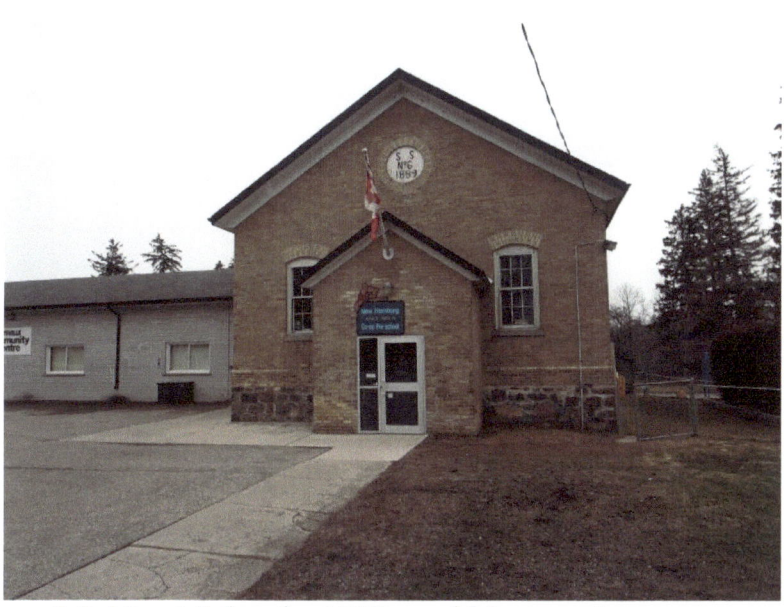

S.S. No. 6 School – 1889 – cobblestone basement
Gothic Revival

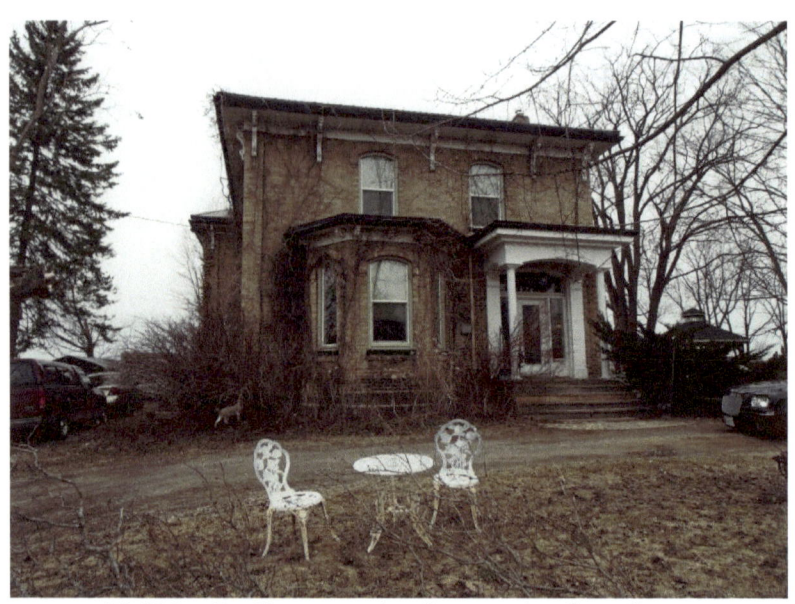

#3426 – Italianate, single cornice brackets,
bay window on ground floor

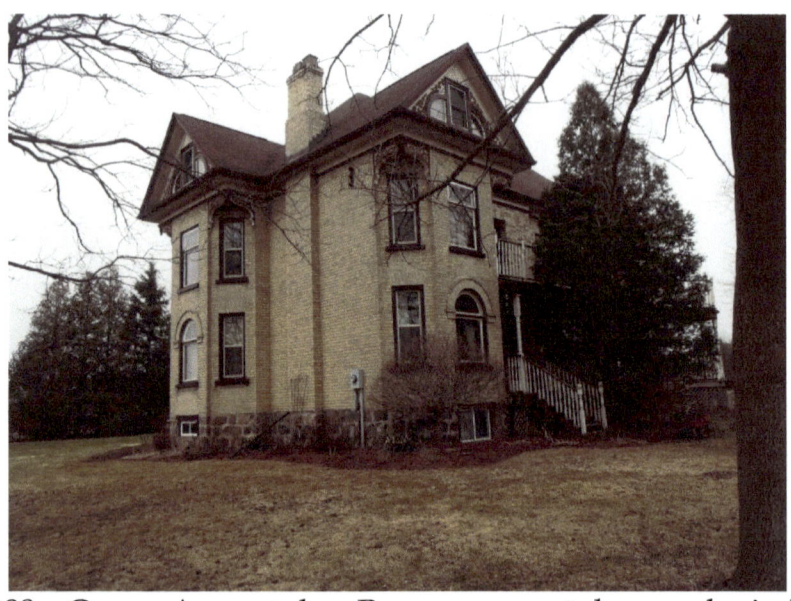

#3398 – Queen Anne style – Romanesque style round window
arches

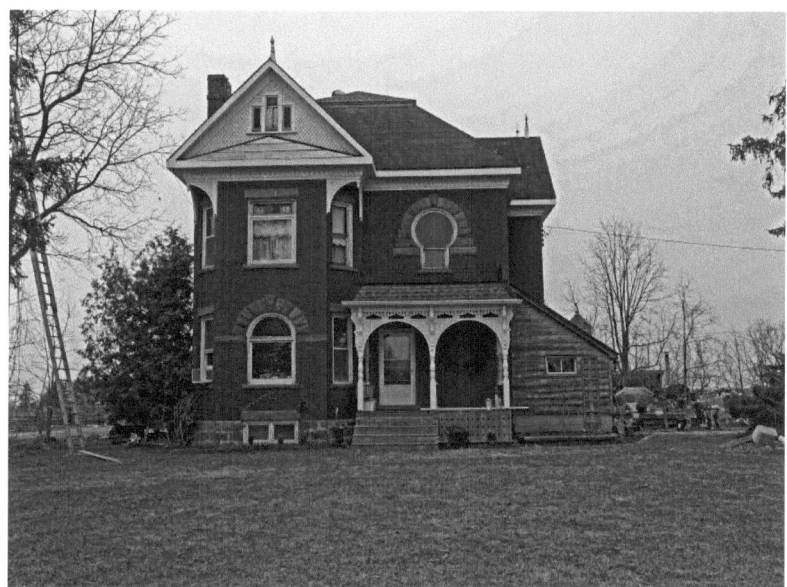

#3330 – Queen Anne features, Palladian window, arched voussoirs, keyhole window, iron cresting above porch

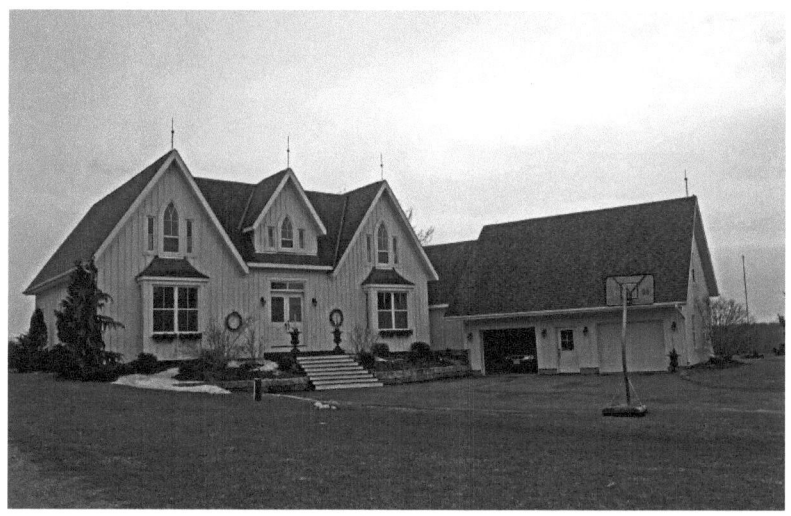

Gothic Revival – dormer between the two gables

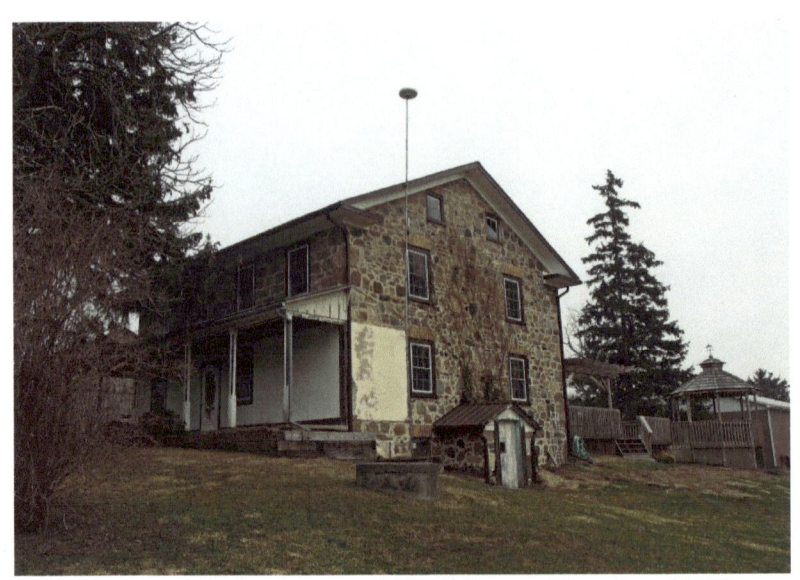

Shantz/Holst house 2653 Huron Road c. 1857
Cobblestone architecture – Gothic Revival style,
cornice return on gable

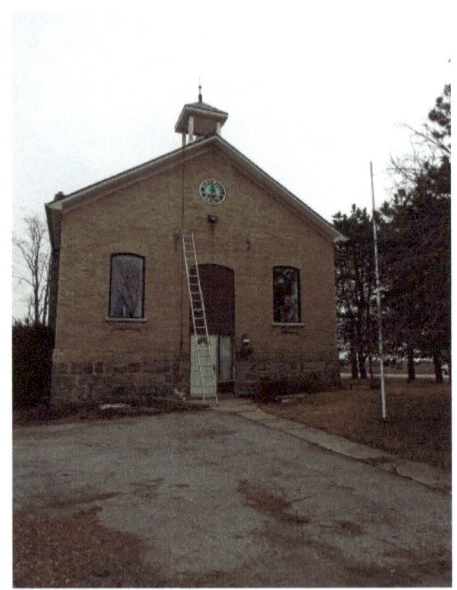

Pinehill School – S.S. #7 – c. 1886 – Gothic Revival

St. Agatha

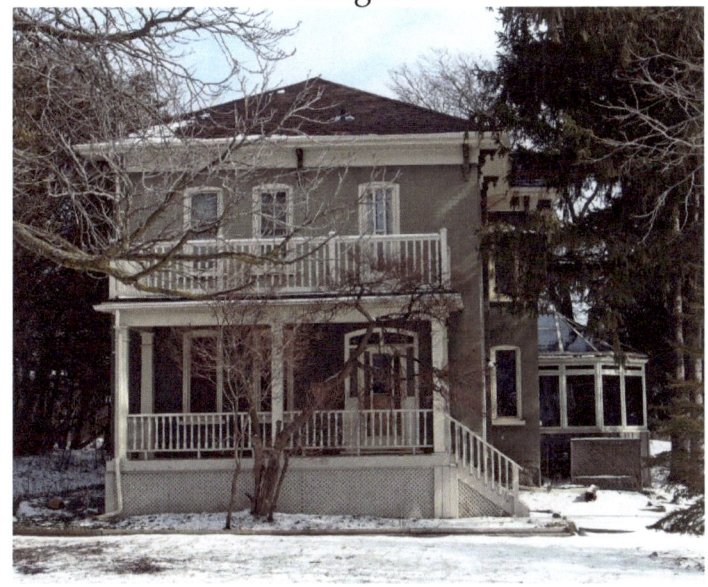

Notre Dame Drive – hipped roof, two-storey, second storey verandah

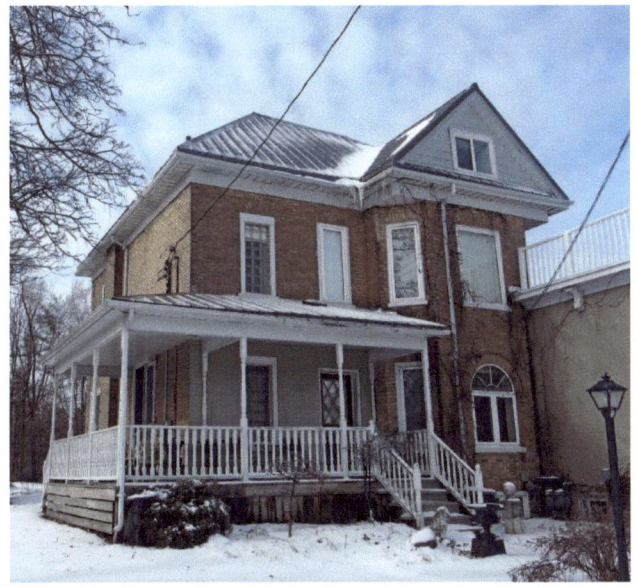

Notre Dame Drive – hipped roof, 2½ storey tower-like bay, wraparound verandah

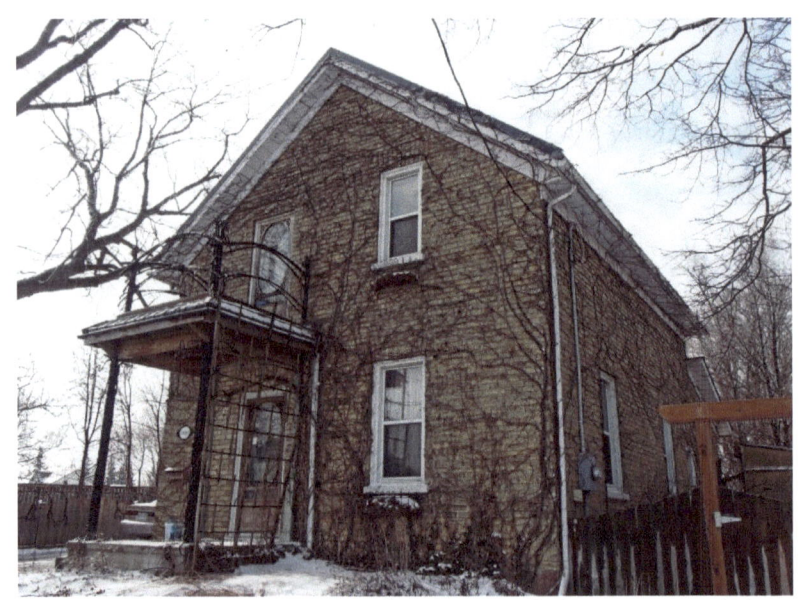

1850 Notre Dame Drive – Gothic Revival, limestone, 1½ storey

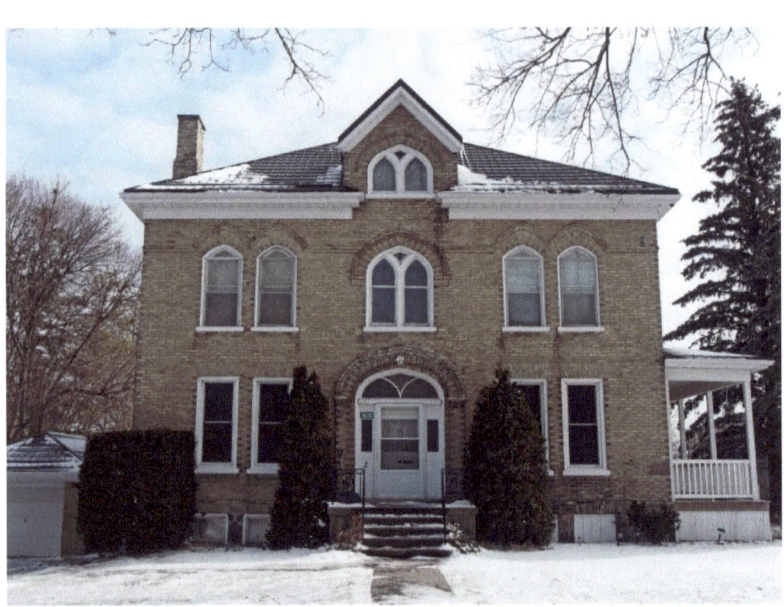

1839 Notre Dame Drive – Georgian style, hipped roof, sidelights and transom around front door

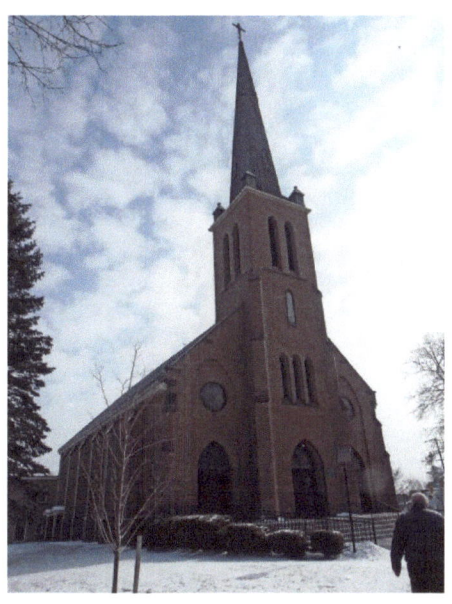

1839 Notre Dame Drive – St. Agatha Catholic Church
Gothic style - constructed in 1899

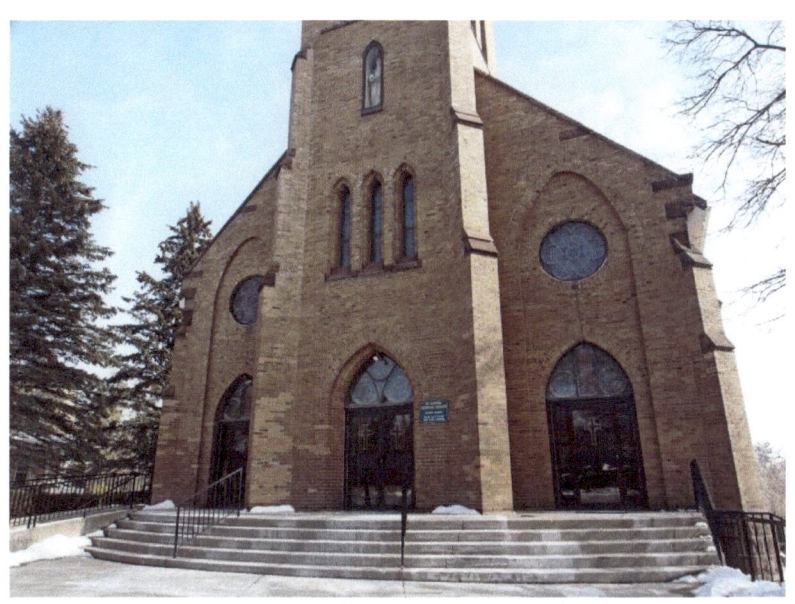

Lancet windows, rose windows

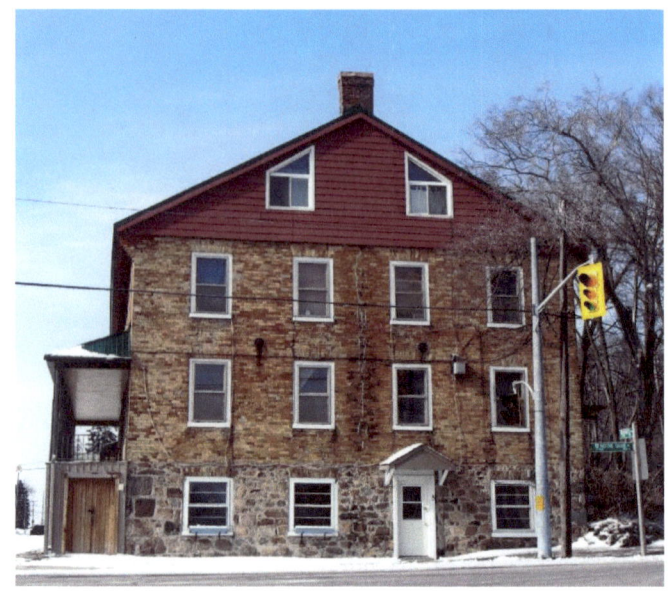

Corner of Notre Dame Drive and Erb's Road
Cobblestone foundation

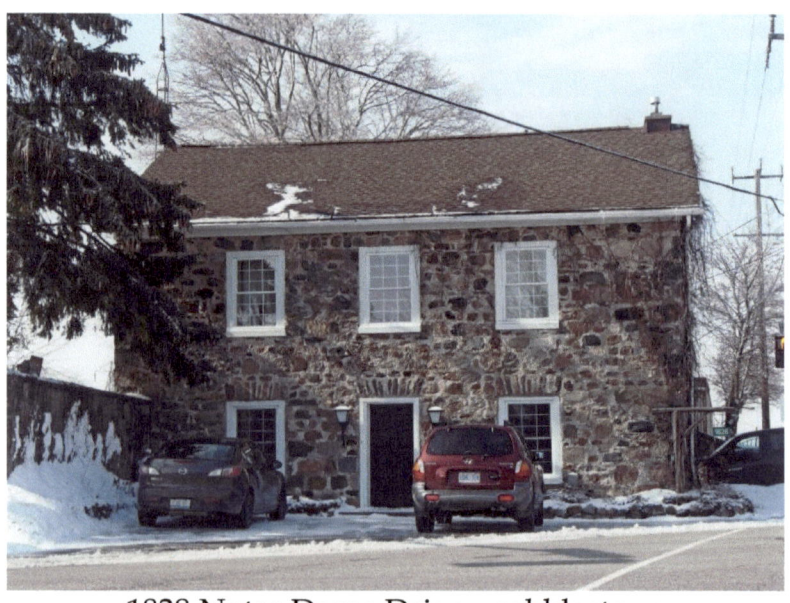

1828 Notre Dame Drive - cobblestone

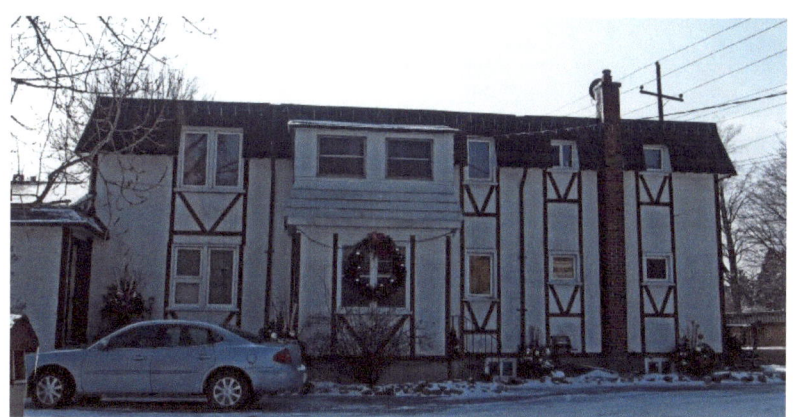

Erb's Road - Tudor

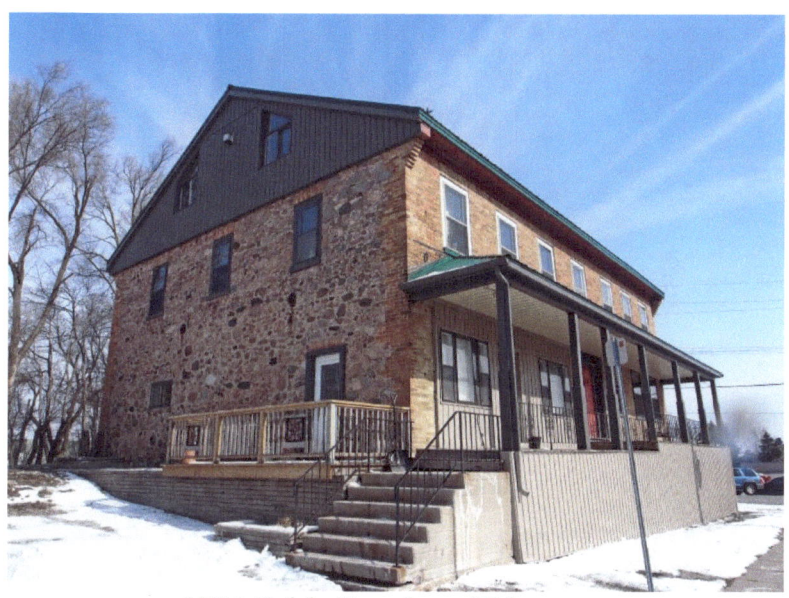

1744 Erb's Road - cobblestone

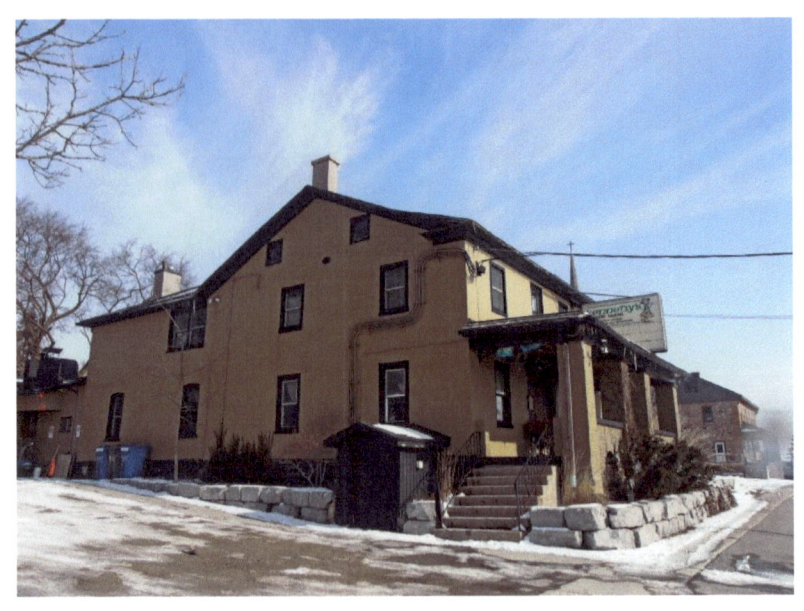

Erb's Road – Kennedy's Country Tavern

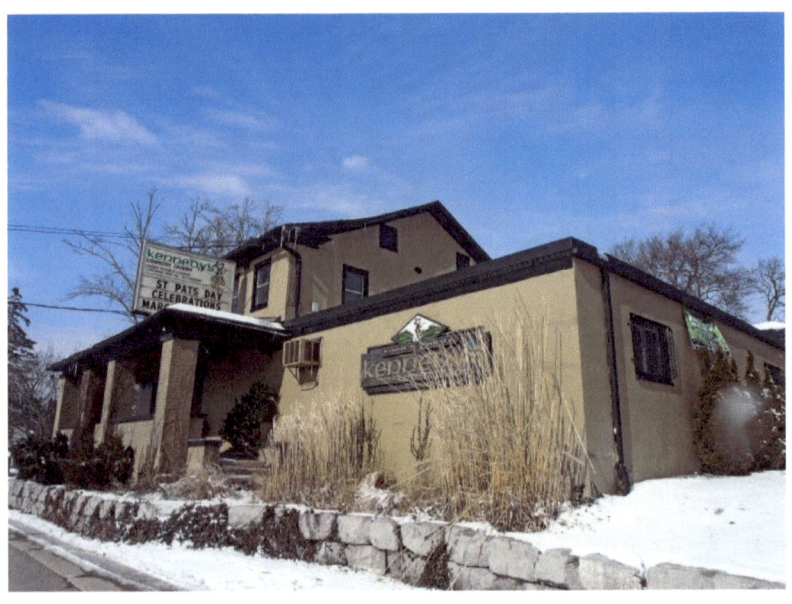

Baden

Baden is a community in the Township of Wilmot in the Regional Municipality of Waterloo. It has a population of less than 1000 and was named after Baden-Baden in Germany. The Baden Tower, a huge television, radio and communications tower, is located on top of one of the Baden Hills. From here CKCO-TV transmits its signal. Much of the area consists of farmlands and there are pine forests as well. Baden was the hometown of Sir Adam Beck who pioneered hydro-electric power.

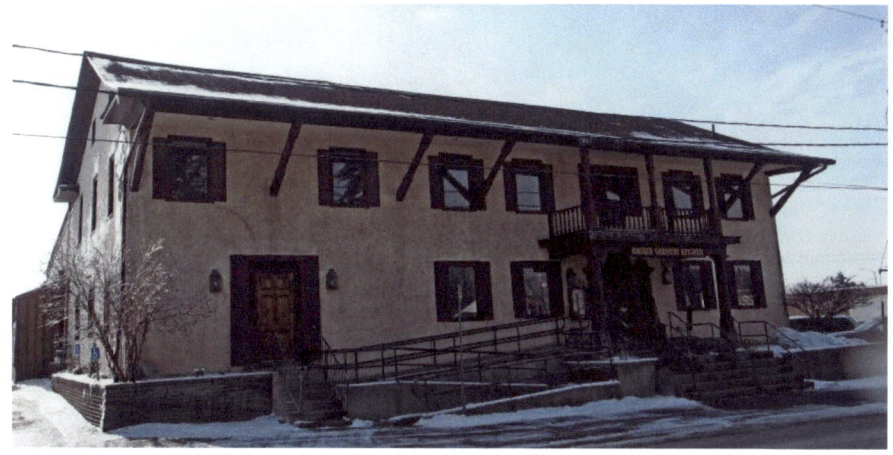

1761 Erb's Road – Angie's Country Kitchen

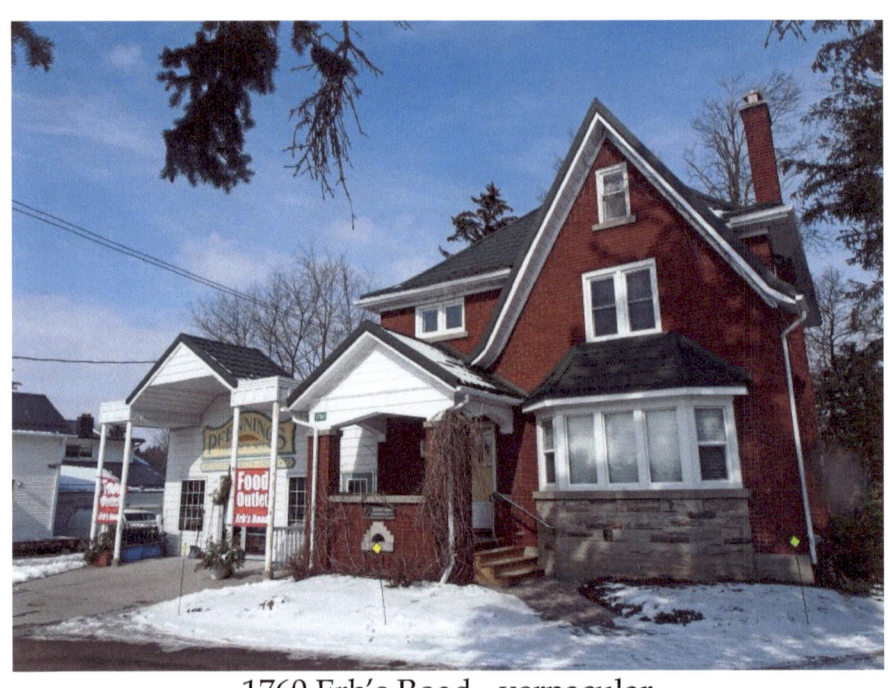

1760 Erb's Road - vernacular

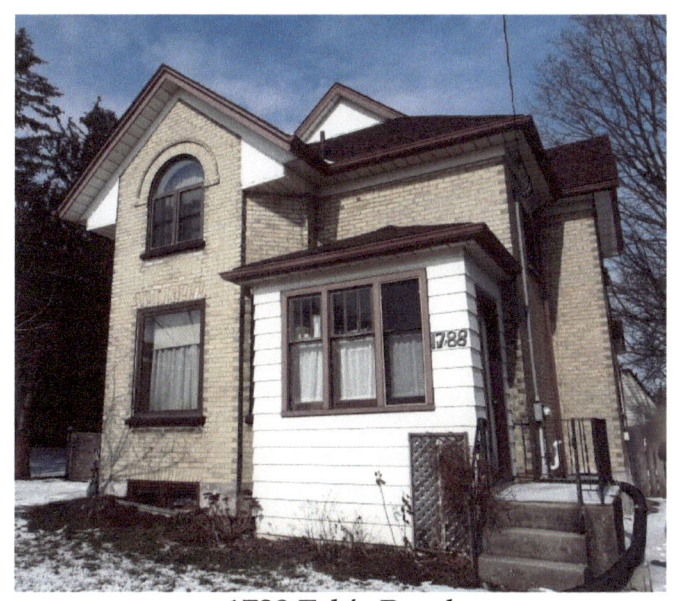

1788 Erb's Road

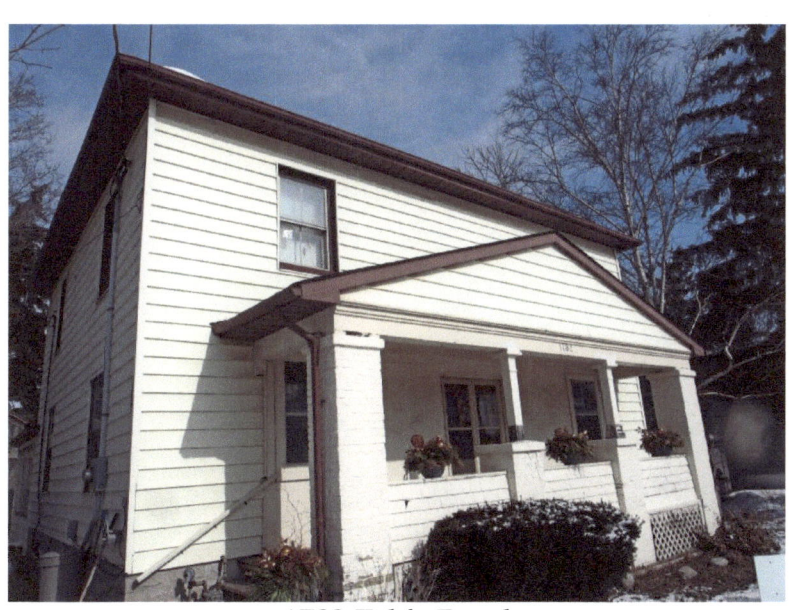

1782 Erb's Road

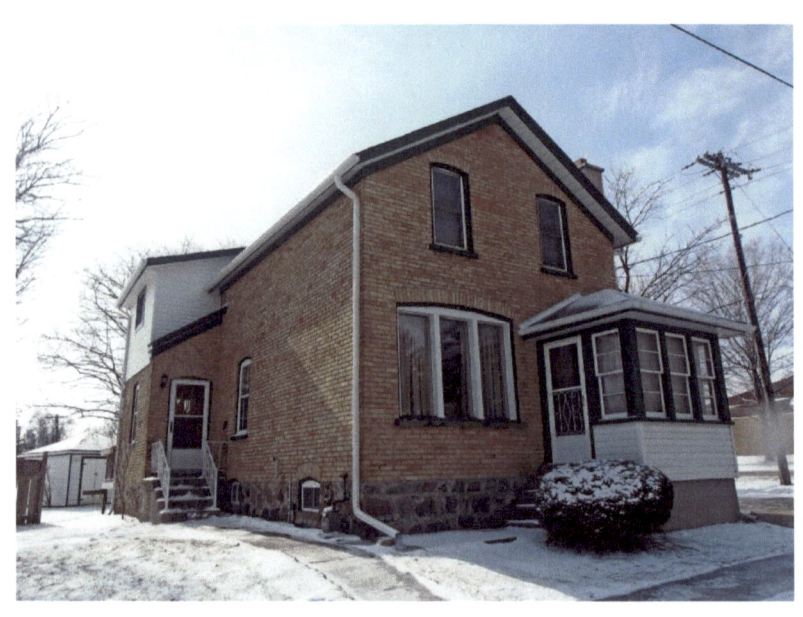

Erb's Road – Gothic Revival

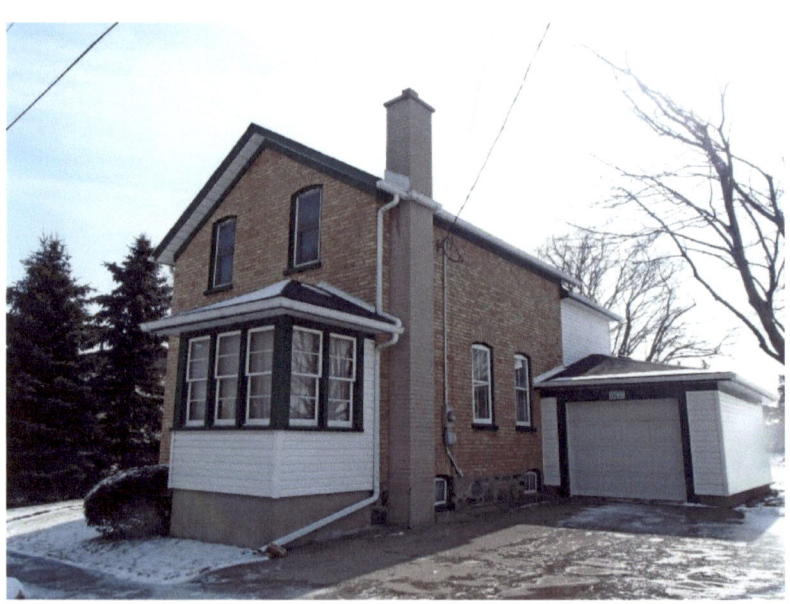

Baden

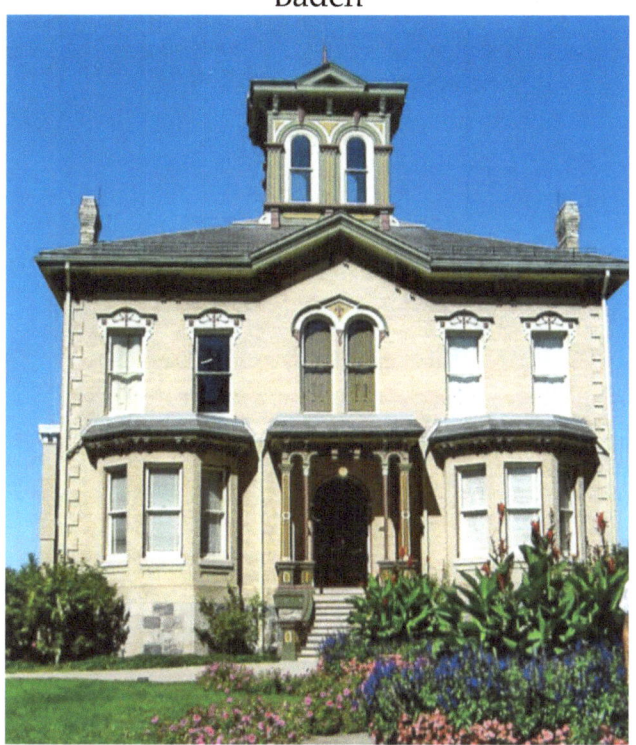

Castle Kilbride is the former residence of James Livingston, a Canadian Member of Parliament and owner of flax and linseed oil mills. It was built in Baden, Ontario in 1877 and named after Livingston's birthplace in Scotland. The house was designed in the Italianate style of architecture and capped with a belvedere lookout.   The major feature of Castle Kilbride is the interior decorative murals in the style of the Italian Renaissance. The trompe l'oeil technique used in the murals gives the illusion of a third dimension.

Castle Kilbride served the Livingston family for three generations from 1877 to 1988, when the family made the decision to sell the home. In 1994, the Castle opened its doors to the public for the first time as a museum after being restored.

Architectural Terms

Bay Window: a window that projects out from a wall in a semicircular, rectangular, or polygonal design, used frequently in Gothic and Victorian designs. Example: 166 Jacob Street	
Brackets: a decorative or weight-bearing structural element which forms a right angle with one side against a wall and the other under a projecting surface such as an eave or roof. Example: #3426 Huron Road, Haysville	
Buttress: a masonry structure built against or projecting from a wall which serves to support or reinforce the wall. In Canadian architecture, they are sometimes used for decoration. Example: 23 Church Street	
Capital: The uppermost finish or decoration on a column. Example: 272 Wilmot Street – ionic capital	
Cobblestone architecture: Refers to the use of cobblestones embedded in mortar as a method for erecting walls on houses and commercial buildings. Example: Shantz/Holst House, Huron Road, Haysville	

Cornice: originally the wooden overhang of the roof. With the use of stone, brick, iron and steel, the cornice is any projecting shelf at the top of a ceiling or roof. They can be very decorative. Example: 144 Jacob Street	
Cornice Return: decorative element on the end of a gable. Example: 59 Weber Street	
Dormer: (French for "sleep") a gable end window that pierces through the plane of a sloping roof surface to create usable space in the top floor or attic of a building by adding headroom. Example: 16 Church Street	
Finial: ornament added to the top of a gable, pinnacle, canopy or spire – a Gothic element. Example: 305 Wilmot Street	
Fretwork: interlaced decorative design resembling a bracket Example: 119 Jacob Street	

Gable: the triangular portion of a wall between the edges of a sloping roof. Example: 191 Jacob Street	
Hipped Roof: a roof where all sides slope downwards to the walls with no gables. Example: 131 Jacob Street	
Lancet Window: a tall, narrow window with a pointed arch at its top. Example: 23 Church Street	
Palladian Window: a large window that is divided into three sections with the centre section larger than the two side sections and usually arched. Example: 141 Jacob Street	
Pediment: a triangular section above the horizontal structure (entablature), typically supported by columns. The inside of the triangle is called the tympanum. Example: 198 Jacob Street	
Vergeboards: also called bargeboards – hang from the projecting end of a roof and are often elaborately carved and ornamented. Example: 305 Wilmot Street	

New Hamburg's Building Styles

Edwardian, 1900-1930 – This style bridges the ornate and elaborate styles of the Victorian era and the simplified styles of the 20th century. Balanced facades, simple roof lines, dormer windows, large front porches, and smooth brick surfaces are its characteristics. Example: 170 Jacob Street	
Gothic Revival, 1830-1890 – These decorative buildings have sharply-pitched gables with highly detailed vergeboards, pointed-arch window openings, and dichromatic brickwork. It is a common style in Ontario. Examples: 198 Jacob Street	
Italianate, 1850-1900 – It has wide-bracketed eaves, belvederes, wrap-around verandahs. Example: 144 Jacob Street	
Regency Cottage, 1830-1860 – This style originated in England in 1815 and spread to Ontario later in the 19th century as British officers retired to Canada. It is a modest one-storey house with a low-pitched hip roof and has a symmetrical front façade. Example: 131 Jacob Street	
Romanesque Revival, 1880-1910 – This style hearkens back to medieval architecture of the 11th and 12th centuries with a heavy appearance, blocky towers and rounded arches. Example: 201 Jacob Street – Romanesque style window arch	

Series Name: Cruising Ontario, Saving Our History One Photo at a Time in colour photos

Books Available in Alphabetical Order:
Aberfoyle, Acton, Ajax, Alton, Amherstburg, Ancaster, Arthur, Auburn, Aylmer, Ayr, Beaver Valley, Belfountain, Belgrave, Belleville, Bloomingdale, Blyth, Brantford, Brockville, Burford, Burgessville, Burlington, Caledon, Caledonia, Cambridge, Carlow, Cayuga, Chatsworth, Cheltenham, Clifford, Colborne, Collingwood, Conestogo, Delhi, Dorchester to Aylmer, Drayton, Drumbo, Dundas, Dunlop, Dunnville, Eden Mills, Elmira, Elora, Embro, Erin, Essex, Fergus, Fort Erie, Georgetown, Goderich, Grimsby, Guelph, Hagersville, Haldimand County, Halton Hills, Hamilton, Hanover, Harriston, Hespeler, Ingersoll, Inglewood, Innerkip, Jarvis, Kingston, Kingsville, Kitchener, Lake Superior, Lincoln, Linwood, Listowel, London, Lucknow, Merrickville, Mono, Mount Brydges, Mount Forest, Mount Pleasant, Neustadt, New Hamburg, Newboro, Newport, Niagara-on-the-Lake, Niagara Falls, North Bay, Norwich, Oakville, Onondaga, Orangeville, Orillia, Oshawa, Otterville, Owen Sound, Palmerston, Paris, Parry Sound, Pelham, Perth, Peterborough, Petrolia, Pickering, Port Colborne, Port Elgin, Port Hope, Port Perry, Portland, Preston, Rockwood, Sarnia, Sault Ste. Marie, Seaforth, Sheffield, Shelburne, Simcoe, Smiths Falls, Smithville, Southampton, Southwest Oxford, St. Catharines, St. George, St. Jacobs, St. Marys, St. Thomas, Stoney Creek, Stouffville, Stratford, Strathroy, Sudbury, Tavistock, Terra Cotta, Thamesford, Thunder Bay, Tillsonburg, Toronto, Uxbridge, Waterdown, Waterford, Waterloo, Welland, Wellesley, West Flamborough, Westport, Whitby, Windsor, Wingham, Woodstock, York, Zorra

Other Books by Barbara Raue

Coins of Gold
Arrows, Indians and Love
The Life and Times of Barbara
The Cromwell Family Book
Laura Secord Discovered
Daddy Where Are You?

Montana Series
Book 1: Montana Dream
Book 2: Life on the Montana Frontier
Book 3: Montana to Boston and Back
Book 4: Montana Sons Go to War
Book 5: Montana Sons Return from War

Book 1: Rite of Passage
Book 2: Rite of Marriage

This is a link to Barbara's website to view all of her books
http://barbararaue.ca

Series Name: Cruising Canada
Saving Our History One Photo at a Time
in colour photos

Book 1-9: Winnipeg Manitoba
Book 10: Osoyoos, B.C.
Book 11: Vernon, Salmon Arm
Book 12: Kelowna
Book 13: Penticton
Book 14: Hope
Book 15-17: Kamloops
Book 18-22: Vancouver
Book 23-25: Victoria
Book 26: Summerland
Book 27: Okanagan Falls, Naramata and Kaleden
Book 28: Chemainus

www.ingramcontent.com/pod-product-compliance
Lightning Source LLC
Chambersburg PA
CBHW040923180526
45159CB00002BA/583